INTUITIVE DESIGN

Eight Steps to an Intuitive UI

Everett N. McKay

Intuitive Design: Eight Steps to an Intuitive UI, First Edition
by Everett N. McKay

©2018 Everett McKay. All rights reserved.

No part of this work may be reproduced or transmitted in any form without the prior written authorization of Black Watch Publishing unless the copying is expressly permitted by federal copyright law.

ISBN-13: 978-0-9996125-0-7

Library of Congress Catalog Card Number: 2018900553

Project Editor: Devon Musgrave
Copyeditor: Devon Musgrave
Interior Designer and Composition: Rob Nance
Illustrator: Jodi Hersh
Cover Design: Jodi Hersh

About the cover

* For intuitive UI, if it looks like a duck and quacks like a duck, make sure it's a duck. Anything else would be unintuitive.

BLACK WATCH PUBLISHING
Manu Forti

PO Box 180
Saint Albans Bay, Vermont 05481

To my clients and students

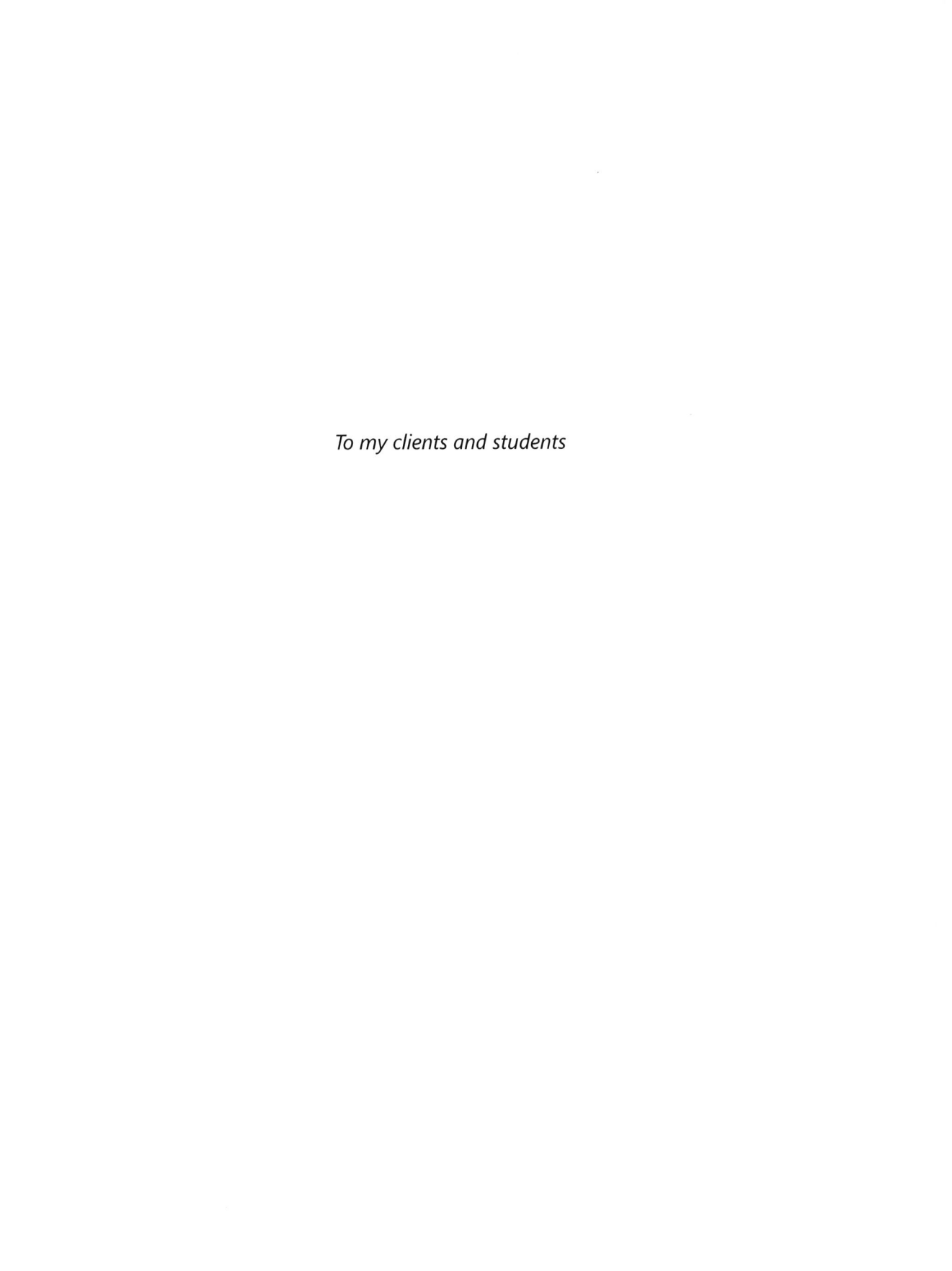

Contents

Acknowledgments xi
Foreword xiii
Why you need to read this book xv

Chapter 1 Why intuitive UIs are important   1

Remember WordPerfect? 1
Goodbye RTFM 2
The world has changed! 3
Managers: Don't bother calculating UX ROI 3
Good UX to great UX 5
The top (weak) excuses 6
The "people can learn" excuse 8
What you need to succeed 10
Summary 11
Exercises 11

Chapter 2 The definition of intuitive UI   13

Some popular but unhelpful definitions 13
A practical definition 15
Not the dictionary definition 16
The manifestation of intuitive UI 16
Is this intuitive? 17
Intuitive UIs are not dumbed down 19
Summary 20
Exercises 21

My answers. 21

Chapter 3 The Eight Attributes of Intuitive UI   23

The interaction lifecycle. 23

The Eight Attributes of Intuitive UI. 24

1 Discoverability. 27

Provide an obvious starting point. 27

Unintuitive: Poor presentation. 29

Unintuitive: Poor location and layout. 29

Unintuitive: Poor recognition. 30

Unintuitive: Too many competing options. 31

Unintuitive: Just plain hard to find, like a puzzle 32

2 Affordance. 33

Obvious always wins 36

The need for labels. 37

3 Comprehensibility. 40

Speaking the target user's language. 40

Meeting expectations 42

Appropriate use of icons. 43

Self-explanatory labels. 43

Asking questions users know the answers to 45

4 Responsive feedback 47

Interaction feedback 47

Status feedback. 48

5 Predictability. 50

Unintuitive: Flat-out wrong. 50

Unintuitive: Misunderstanding. 51

Unintuitive: Undesired side effects 53

6 Efficiency 55

Unintuitive: Inefficient interaction. 55

Unintuitive: Unnecessary interaction 57
Appropriate defaults 58
Unintuitive: Forgetting or not using user input 61
Error handling 62
Appropriate constraints 63
Unintuitive: Technical failure 64
Unintuitive: Unnecessary restrictions/annoyances 66
Unintuitive: Contextual stupidity 67

7 Forgiveness 69
Preventing mistakes 69
Undo 73
Easy recovery 74

8 Explorability 76
Confirm destructive actions 76
Direct manipulation vs. accidental manipulation 77
User in control 78
Clear navigation models 78
Clear commit models 79
Building confidence 80

Is this intuitive? 82

Building an intuitive UI 84

Summary 88

Exercises 88

My answers 90

Chapter 4 Bonus intuitive UI attributes 93

Familiar 93

Consistent 97

Learnable 101

Invisible 102

Being intuitive in stressful situations 104

Digestible 106

Let's ditch the metaphors too! 106

Summary 107

Exercises 107

My answers 108

Chapter 5 Strategically unintuitive   109

The cost of intuitive 109

The Seven Good Reasons for Unintuitive UI 112

Shortcuts and gestures 115

Games and puzzles are different 119

The Levels of Intuitiveness chart 119

Single-trial learning 122

The definition of *intuitive UI*, revisited 123

Scoring tips 124

What about onboarding and coach marks? 125

Strategically unintuitive 128

Everett's Law of Intuitive UI 129

Summary 129

Exercises 129

My answers 130

Chapter 6 Intuitive task flows   133

The task lifecycle 133

The trouble with task flows 136

Inductive UI 136

Explainable first 138

Designing main instructions 139

Designing page integrity 141

Working through two examples 144
      Design Challenge 1: A tool for web developers 144
      Design Challenge 2: Configuring a virtual machine 145

When to *not* display a main instruction 145

What about responsive design? 148

Summary. 150

Exercises 150

Answers. 151
      Design Challenge 1: A tool for web developers 151
      Design Challenge 2: Configuring a virtual machine 152

Chapter 7   A design process for intuitive UI   153

Maximizing the value of usability testing 153

A process for making intuitive design decisions 154

Grading intuitiveness 156

The Seven Levels of UX Persuasion 157

A real-world persuasion scenario. 159

Traditional heuristic evaluations 160

Modern heuristic evaluations 161

Streamlined Cognitive Walkthroughs 163

Usability testing. 166

The User Manual Highlighter Test 168

Summary. 170

Exercises 170

Conclusion 171
Glossary 173
Index 179
About the Author 185
About UX Design Edge 187
Got Feedback? 189
Get the Intuitive Design Heuristics Playing Cards! 191
The *Intuitive Design* Store 193

Acknowledgments

Every book has a backstory, and they all share one thing in common: the author's gratitude to all those who helped make it happen—sometimes unknowingly. That help is essential for inspiration, telling the right story, getting things done, and getting the details right.

If there is a backstory theme for this book, it's that one thing leads to another. I actually didn't intend to write this book—at the start I had a completely different subject in mind—but events that occurred over a decade somehow conspired to lead me here.

This first event was meeting **Jan Miksovsky** in 2004 while both of us were on the Windows team at Microsoft. Jan invented a new design concept called Inductive User Interface (IUI) and presented the concept to my team. This was the first step in a long journey that helped me realize that UI design is ultimately a form of human communication (leading to my last book *UI Is Communication*), which started my deep thinking about intuitive UI. I'm thrilled that Jan graciously agreed to write this book's Foreword.

The next significant event occurred in 2016. I was recording a class on intuitive UI design when it occurred to me that I should have a poster to visually explain what I was calling the Eight Steps to Intuitive UI. I gave a rough draft to my amazing visual designer **Jodi Hersh**, who quickly created the Eight Steps to an Intuitive UI poster that shows the intuitive attributes in a fun, approachable way. This poster proved very popular—I would bring dozens and later hundreds of copies to conferences and quickly run out.

The next significant event, logically anyway, actually occurred a few months before the poster during one of my classes. One of my students, **Raffaele Limosani**, gave me valuable feedback on how to improve the class. Among the feedback was his disappointment that I didn't hand out copies of my UI Is Communication book in the class. I had rejected that idea many times in the past simply because the costs were prohibitive—even for eBooks—as traditional publishers don't give authors the discounts you might assume. Raffaele's feedback inspired me to self-publish my next book to have the flexibility to do whatever I want, and was a major turning point in this project.

I was about to start a rather ambitious book on another topic when it occurred to me that it would be wise to do something simpler for my first self-published book. I thought, "Something like the Eight Steps to an Intuitive UI would be perfect!" And with that, this book was conceived. All by chance: a presentation, a poster, some feedback, an impulse—and Bob's your uncle!

This book would not be what it is without the fantastic editorial skills of **Devon Musgrave**. An excellent editor has the amazing ability to take your rough text and turn it into exactly what you meant to say—had you been a better writer. **Rob Nance** masterfully created the interior design and did the page layout, paging, production, and publication. **Jodi Hersh** did an extraordinary job creating the Eight Steps poster and book cover, plus the illustrations and mockups.

The book would also be lacking without the fantastic feedback I received from my reviewers. Many thanks to **Jan Miksovsky**, **Kent Sullivan**, **Jonathan Walter**, **William Key**, **Jörgen Normark**, **Mike Donahue**, **Nicole Maynard**, **Erk Ekin**, **Noah Patullo**, **Vinny Pasceri**, **Sam Thompson,** and **William Shellenberger** for reading my drafts and going the extra mile to give constructive feedback. They found all the mistakes and helped ensure everything made sense, while keeping me honest. Finally, thanks to **Dr. Gyles Morrison**, **Dr. Jennifer Cham**, **Marie Seguin**, **Michele McKay**, **Phil McKay**, and **Ümit Koca** for help with miscellaneous artwork.

Foreword

In 2011, engineer and entrepreneur Marc Andreessen summarized the unstoppable spread of software into every industry by stating, "Software is eating the world." If that software is to be any good, it must be well-designed. Until the day comes when the design task itself can be substantially automated, we will need more and more people who can design software well. That requires good materials for teaching the craft of software design, such as this book you are now reading.

I first met Everett McKay in the early 2000s when we worked together on a version of Microsoft Windows. At a time when the software industry was fascinated with tricking out user interfaces with spectacular visual effects, Everett was drawn to the humbler task of studying software that could be explained to the user—or, ideally, which *explained itself* to the user. The world has moved on from the visual effects in fashion at that time, but the need for intuitive, self-explanatory software is as durable as ever.

The fundamental challenge in software design is how to simultaneously conceive of a novel, complex system while seeing clearly how that system might be perceived by an uninitiated user. In the very act of conception, you move yourself towards a deeper understanding but away from the novice's perspective. This makes it harder and harder for you to imagine how a new user might experience your design.

Fortunately, you can learn and practice techniques for putting yourself back into the mind of a user. This book presents a number of such techniques, and they can help guide you to better design decisions. Usability testing, for example, is a critical tool for letting you see how actual users fare with a design. Better still, you can try to spot problems earlier in the design process with tools such as a group cognitive walkthrough. Still earlier, you might employ Everett's unique and insightful taxonomy for self-grading the intuitiveness of a design.

One tool which both Everett and I have found enormously useful is articulating the main instruction that should (or could) be used to label a page or window in a user interface. I developed that technique, which I called inductive user interface design, in the mid-1990s while leading the design team for a personal finance product. It struck me that many times a designer would incorporate a title or label in their designs for a page or window, but they would use entirely different words when called upon to explain the same design in person. Invariably, when explaining things in person, the designer would use *better* words.

Designers sometimes use jargon, stilted language, or ambiguous terms when adding text to a screen. But when talking through that design with a colleague, they use more natural and familiar language. Significantly, when asked to explain the interface to a novice, they try very hard to think about what the novice might or might not understand and they take pains to explain things in terms of the novice's likely goals. It turns out that trying to explain something to a novice is such a compelling exercise that you can benefit from it even when you don't have a novice in front of you. Simply imagining what you would say—or better, trying to say the words out loud—can be enough to trigger an empathetic insight that leads to a better explanation. You can capitalize on that effect, working towards a better design that either incorporates the explanation or, ideally, is so self-evident that the explanation can be omitted from the screen.

Familiarizing yourself with such techniques, and using them regularly in your design practice, can make you a more effective designer. We're never so experienced that we can't find use for new tools. Whether you are just starting out or have been designing software for a number of years, you will find tools here that should find a place in your designer's toolbox.

Jan Miksovsky
Seattle, WA
January 2018

Why you need to read this book

Any UI's unintuitiveness diminishes me, because I am involved in design. [Inspired by John Donne]

It's surprising to realize that our profession hasn't adequately grappled with such a fundamental concept as intuitive design. The traditional user-centered design process treats intuitive design as something unpredictable that can be discovered, eventually, only through significant amounts of usability testing and iteration. This makes the design process feel aimless rather than deliberate. Worse, using this approach requires time, patience, and resources that most software teams—let's be honest—don't have. **If intuitive design were just a matter of common sense, why is there so much unintuitive UI in the world?** You can tell when designers have abandoned hope when they refer to "intuitive" with air quotes or argue that unintuitive UIs are just fine. We need to raise our game!

We are living in an increasingly agile world. Two-week Scrum sprints mean fast design cycles. **You need to make good decisions in less-than-ideal circumstances. You need to get it right—or at least close to right—quickly, the first time.**

Who is this book for?

Intuitive Design is for anyone who wants to design intuitive UIs. To guide you to that end, it will teach you

- what it means for a UI to be intuitive,
- what attributes are required to make a UI intuitive,
- multiple tools and techniques for creating and evaluating intuitiveness,
- how to determine when it's acceptable for a UI to not be intuitive, and
- how to effectively persuade team members, managers, stakeholders, and clients that a UI is or is not intuitive.

Do you need to read this book? Here's a simple test: Can you take a variety of unintuitive UI elements, precisely determine their design problems, determine whether those problems really need to be improved (vs. better left as is), determine exactly how to fix them, and persuasively explain your recommendations to others?

I find that even highly experienced designers find this test challenging—especially the last step. We can find the problems, but we lack confidence in our solutions and have a very difficult time convincing others. Aside from usability testing, we lack a framework for analyzing designs and an objective, actionable vocabulary for convincing others. **Those are the very tools that this book will provide you.**

Being persuasive—and getting teams beyond personal opinion

When you think about it, everything you do as a designer requires some sort of approval. You must convince your team, managers, developers, stakeholders, and clients, so your design work is affected by your ability to sell your ideas. The awful truth is that great design doesn't always sell itself and even if you are an experienced designer, your opinion isn't always persuasive. Why? Because everyone assumes their opinion is better than yours. **If you want your best work to be acknowledged and used, you need to sell your ideas more objectively.**

Tweet This!

Suppose someone on your team were to tell you that your design proposal was unintuitive. Many designers respond defensively: "What's intuitive is subjective. I think the design is intuitive and you think it's not, so we have to agree to disagree." Such discussions accomplish nothing; we're just talking past each other. Design feedback, no matter how astute, is usually met with resistance and requires persuasion, and discussing platitudes like "Don't make me think" doesn't get us very far. (And reading this book will help you understand what "don't make me think" really means.)

The word *intuitive* is vague and abstract, but the Eight Attributes of Intuitive UI (defined in Chapter 3) are specific, concrete, and measurable. You and your team will have much more productive conversations by using these attributes. If you tell me my design is unintuitive, we can argue about it. But if you say that a feature in my design isn't *discoverable* in a particular context or that its *affordance* is misleading, I know exactly what you're saying and what to do about it. **We are no longer having a subjective conversation about abstract concepts—we're discussing specific, concrete design problems!**

You need this book so that you can make better design decisions and be more persuasive when making the case for those decisions. And you need everyone on your team working with the same design thinking and speaking the same language, so share your copy or give everyone their own copy. Consider giving a copy to your managers and clients with a note saying, "This is what I do!" **Reading this book will enable your team and clients to communicate more effectively, argue less, and work toward the same goal: truly intuitive design.**

How to read this book

I know you're busy and I value your time, so I've designed this book to be scannable. While I would love for you to read it from cover to cover, **if you are in a hurry and want to get the gist of a chapter, just read the headings, the examples and their captions, the bits in bold, and the summary at the end.** This will give you the crucial content, and you can return later for the details when you need them.

The chapters are intended to be read in order, but doing so isn't a requirement. **You can get the gist of the book by scanning Chapters 2, 3, 5, and 6.** If a section refers to material from another chapter, I call that out explicitly for you. **The glossary summarizes the book's terminology so that you can quickly look up important words as necessary.**

To help you scan the examples, many have margin icons to help you quickly determine whether the example is intuitive. **Here are the margin icons and their meaning:**

An example of intuitive design.

An example of unintuitive design.

An example of strategically unintuitive design (defined in Chapter 5).

What's not here

What's not in a book is every bit as revealing as what is. What's here: a practical definition of *intuitive* plus the Eight Attributes of Intuitive UI, based on design principles and the interaction lifecycle. **What isn't here? The wonky, academic material on intuitive UI that you often find elsewhere.** There are no discussions of human psychology, conceptual models, physical and cultural environments, activity theory, or magic escalators. These are all potential factors (and have influenced the material I'm presenting), but in many cases, they are secondary and focusing on them tends to confuse more than clarify.

My goal is to keep the concepts as simple and practical as possible. If you want your design discussions to focus on user psychology, cognitive load, and user models, feel free—but by applying the concepts in this book, you can skip all that without losing much.

UI vs. UX

Not everyone defines *UI* and *UX* the same way, so let me give you my definitions to avoid confusion.

I define UI (user interface) as what users see, hear, and possibly feel on the device, plus how they interact with it. UX (user experience) is that, plus everything else the product touches—from the purchasing, out-of-box, configuration, daily-usage, and support experiences, to experiences that don't even involve interaction, such as defaults or automatic behaviors. CX (customer experience) is defined even more broadly to include the entire customer relationship, especially with respect to the customer journey, satisfaction, loyalty, and branding. **Here's a simple, 99% accurate test: if you can easily sketch it, it's UI; if you can't, it's UX.** My definitions match Don Norman's (YouTube: *Don Norman: The Term "UX"*), who is credited with coining the term user experience.

Given these definitions, I refer to intuitive UI because I am specifically referring to users' interaction with the product—and not anything beyond that. While it's not incorrect to refer to an intuitive user experience, it is less precise.

This is a mobile-first book—not a retrofit

We live in a mobile world with diverse platforms and interaction models, so I've used a *mobile-first* approach for this book. I assume that you're likely designing for mobile users using mobile apps or responsive websites on mobile devices, often with touch-based interactions—apps and sites that need to work well on desktop too. (I also assume that you're reading this book on a mobile device!) **I use mostly mobile examples and mobile language: the product you are designing is an** *app*, **and users** *tap the screen* **as the most fundamental interaction.** Of course, these assumptions aren't always accurate—your product could be a desktop app, desktop website, or hardware control panel, and the user could be using a desktop or laptop, typing with a keyboard, clicking with a mouse, using assistive technologies, or even interacting with a speech-based device through voice alone. So, *mobile-first* doesn't mean *mobile-exclusive*—I do refer to some non-mobile interactions here and there. **Rest assured that the concepts and principles in this book can be applied to all devices and interaction models.**

Why I wrote this book

Although I've delivered many classes and workshops to UX design professionals, **my specialty is to teach UX design to non-designers—especially to software developers and managers.** Being a software developer myself who learned UX design "the hard way" (trial and a lot of error), **I have a special appreciation for what developers, managers, and other technical people respond to.**

I teach and consult on a wide range of UX design areas—everything from mobile design to software branding—but my favorite UX subjects are those that initially appear to be the most vague and subjective. I believe, however, that UX design is a principled, objective practice, not a subjective art. **My mission is to take as much personal opinion and subjectivity out of UX design as possible.** I've been very satisfied in my success with that mission.

No design subject is currently more personal and subjective than what it means for a UI to be intuitive. People frequently tell me, "An intuitive UI is personal and subjective. What I find intuitive, you might not, and vice versa." They insist that it's impossible to know whether a UI is intuitive without performing extensive usability testing. I find that perspective unsatisfying because **I know that we can assess intuitiveness through clear design principles.** But to be clear, these principles aren't a substitute for usability testing but a way to make the testing we do much more effective.

Tweet This!

My initial research on intuitive UI was surprisingly unproductive. I went through my tall stack of UI design books and looked up "intuitive" in each index. You would think such an

Why you need to read this book   **xix**

obvious topic would be addressed in every design book, but, surprisingly, only Jef Raskin's *The Humane Interface* had a definition. Raskin defines *intuitive* to mean *familiar*:

> *One of the most laudatory terms used to describe an interface is to say that it is "intuitive." When examined closely, this concept turns out to vanish like a pea in a shell game and be replaced with the more ordinary but accurate term "familiar."*

Familiar? We have replaced one abstract term with another. What exactly does *familiar* mean? How can we use *familiar* to evaluate a design? I'm not convinced that Raskin's alternative definition is a step up in accuracy or practicality.

Fortunately, I didn't stop there. **My breakthrough was to realize that designers need a framework for intuitive UI—consisting of a specific definition, a specific set of attributes, and an interaction model to hold everything together.** This framework gives structure and focus. As a result, this book isn't a randomly assembled mishmash of "top UX design things you need to think about."

Intuitive Design explains this intuitive UI framework in detail and applies it to many practical examples, ranging from mobile and desktop apps to everyday things. **At the time of this writing, I have been using this framework for over eight years and the results have been excellent.** No, an intuitive UI isn't personal and subjective—we just need to use a framework that establishes a shared understanding and that makes our assessments of UIs objective and effective.

CHAPTER 1

Why intuitive UIs are important

UI design is an objective, principled form of human communication, not a subjective art!

Remember WordPerfect?

I vividly remember my struggle to learn WordPerfect 5.1 back in the day. (And I'm sure older readers remember this as well—it's hard to forget. Younger readers: Substitute here any app that required watching several YouTube videos to learn.) And "struggle to learn" is the right phrase—learning how to use the app required a significant amount of time and even more motivation. **You couldn't just install the software and use it. You had to read the user manual** or take a training course. WordPerfect was not designed to be intuitive—it was designed to be learned.

But what is most remarkable is that requiring users to learn wasn't remarkable at the time. With a few exceptions, this was the way all software was designed. (The technology industry is full of such products, many of them very successful.) The entrepreneurship process was simple: find an important problem, solve it through technology without worrying about usability, and your highly motivated users will do whatever it takes to learn how to use your solution. **Software executives never had to worry that poor user experiences would result in a loss of sales, because customers expected to need documentation and training.**

FIGURE 1-1 The classic WordPerfect 5.1 user manuals from 1989.

Imagine trying to sell such software today. Or even worse, imagine trying to sell a mobile app that required your customers to read a user manual to be productive. There's only one way I see it happening—through force. If users are required to use an app or no viable alternatives exist, only then will they be willing to "struggle to learn." **This approach to design now works only for highly specialized markets targeting highly specialized users—who typically lack alternatives. For the mainstream market, forget it!**

Goodbye RTFM

Not long ago, it was acceptable to solve significant usability problems through documentation alone. Why bother fixing the underlying design when you can just document the workaround! **This is known as RTFM, or Read The Fine Manual. Users were expected to read the manual, so why waste valuable time improving usability when you could spend that time adding more features instead?** This is clearly old-school thinking. (And if your team is still in that school, you're in trouble!)

This is not to say that modern apps shouldn't have user manuals. **Modern user manuals focus on helping users understand how to get full value out of the product, not on explaining the confusing, hard-to-use, unintuitive UI.** A modern user manual is optional, not required.

By the way, this RTFM thinking doesn't just lead to user manuals. **Manual-dependent UI design also leads to training, technical support, online Help (and associated internet research), poor productivity, and, on occasion, very costly mistakes.** (And yes, watching YouTube videos counts as training.) It leads to poor customer reviews spiced with words like frustrating, confusing, bewildering, clumsy, awkward, and annoying. The need for a user manual is merely the most visible manifestation of a much larger problem.

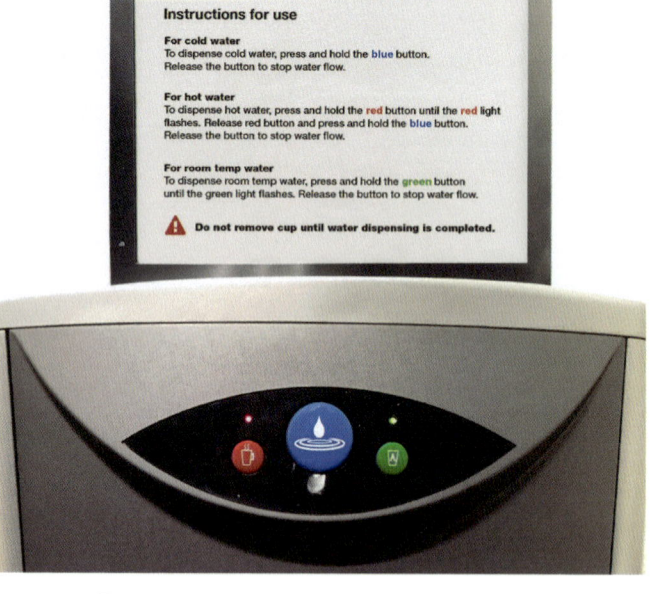

FIGURE 1-2 The need for a user manual is just one manifestation of unintuitive UI. There are many others.

Chapter 1 Why intuitive UIs are important

The world has changed!

FIGURE 1-3 The iPhone has a user manual, but few users know or care because they don't need it. (To find it: Check the bottom of your bookmarks.)

How many user manuals have you read for mobile apps? I'm pretty sure the answer is none! **I strongly believe that mobile apps have permanently changed the UX quality bar.** People are walking around with great user experiences in their pockets—with apps that they can quickly install and get immediate value from—and they now have the same high expectations for the other products they use.

We have a new generation of users, many who have never read a user manual in their life. They grew up without expecting the need for documentation and training. They are your next generation of users. **And don't expect their documentation reading habits to change.**

Tweet This!

> *The design world has changed—there is a new generation of users who won't read user manuals. Modern user manuals are optional and focus on helping users understand how to get full value out of the product.*

FIGURE 1-4 Do you think they read the user manual?

Managers: Don't bother calculating UX ROI

Many managers want their UX teams to demonstrate the ROI (return on investment) of UX design to justify any investment. I understand the need to demonstrate value and effectiveness, but this demand represents old-school thinking because it implies that investing in UX design is optional. In the new school, excellent UX design is mandatory even to be a player!

I don't have much faith in these ROI calculations, but it's not for a lack of trying. I tried using *Cost-Justifying Usability*, by Randolph Bias and Brenda Mayhew, which presents several approaches to calculating the "Net Present Value" of UX investments based on a variety of models and many, many assumptions. These techniques are so complex and assumption-laden that they didn't impress me. But you can use them to come up with a number if you really must.

I prefer a simple, back-of-the-envelope approach that I find more credible for calculating both the need for and the results of UX design investment. If your tech support team tracks their support calls (and they should), make sure they tag the ones related to poor usability, such as confusing error messages. **Determine that technical support cost per year. This is a real, assumption-free number that's likely disturbingly large.** And it's just one of many costs due to poor usability. Make getting that number down part of your UX team's mission and thereby improve customer satisfaction. Your impact will be measurable through the same tech support data.

Still, such ROI numbers miss the point. Great UX design is no longer about getting return on investment—it's about staying in the game! It's about gaining or at least preserving market share and staying relevant to today's users. If your product is harder to use than the competition's, it's game over for getting new users.

In *The Innovator's Dilemma*, Clayton Christensen describes how **disruptive innovations displace established market leaders, often through much simpler solutions.** These new solutions aren't feature-rich—they simply do a better job at the few things users care about the most, eventually eroding the legacy player's market share.

The clear implication: Suppose you are an established player with a market-leading, powerful, feature-rich legacy product that's hard to use and requires substantial documentation and training. **If you have a competitor that is a disruptive innovator, they aren't going to compete with you on features (where you are strong). They are going to attack your poor UX (where you are weak) with a simple, intuitive UI that doesn't require documentation or training.** Such a competitor can turn your legacy product's greatest strength into its greatest weakness.

Tweet This!

For modern software, a better question than "What is the ROI on UX?" is "Do we want to remain competitive?" Harsh news. But don't blame me—I'm not judging, I'm just being honest!

> *Requiring UX design ROI is old school because it presumes that investing in your product's user experience is optional.*

Good UX to great UX

If you need further convincing, **let's look at how well-designed products affect the bottom line.** In his bestselling book, *Good to Great: Why Some Companies Make the Leap and Others Don't*, Jim Collins demonstrates how good companies became great in part through stock price performance. Let compare the stock price of Apple vs. Microsoft starting in 2000:

FIGURE 1-5 Stock performance–wise, Microsoft is good, but Apple is great!

Many factors lie behind this difference in performance, but Apple consistently produces well-designed products that customers love to buy and use. Turns out, that makes a lot of money!

At the time of this writing (2017), people still line up to get into Apple Stores. While I applaud the excitement and loyalty, it makes me wonder if these people have better things to do.

FIGURE 1-6 Did this guy just win the lotto? Nope, he just bought an iPhone. Are your customers this excited about buying your product?

FIGURE 1-7 Attention shoppers: You can buy this stuff online now. Please go home to your families.

The top (weak) excuses

At this point, I hope you're convinced that having an intuitive UI is important to the success of your product. Still, many old-school teams haven't gotten the memo yet and are sticking to their usability-through-RTFM ways.

I've heard all the rationalizations and excuses. Here are some of my favorites:

- **Designing an intuitive UI is impossible because it's personal and subjective!** *I might find a UI to be intuitive and you might not.* This statement is convincing only if you don't understand what intuitive UIs are all about. The top goal of this book is to give you an objective understanding of what makes a UI intuitive. It really isn't a matter of opinion.

- **Our users are highly experienced, trained professionals!** *You can't just walk up and use our product—our users have to be trained. It's not designed for your mom or dad.* Some applications are targeted at trained professionals, but that doesn't give you a free pass to make your designs unintuitive. It turns out that, just like everyone else, highly experienced, trained professionals don't like wasting time or making mistakes with an unintuitive UI. For example, when I'm flying, I certainly want the

  FIGURE 1-8 Yes, airline pilots are highly trained professionals, but for safety's sake I sure hope this cockpit design is intuitive. I don't want pilots having to depend upon memorization or experimentation during critical situations.

  pilots to have plenty of training. But I hope that the training is focused on how to fly the aircraft safely and handle emergency situations, not on understanding what the confusing, unintuitive avionics really mean. Even trained professionals need intuitive UI.

- **This is an internal line-of-business app—our users must use it!** *They don't have a choice, so why bother making it intuitive?* As I suggested earlier, users might be motivated to use an unintuitive app if they are forced, so this claim is at least plausible. But there are two flaws:

  - Unintuitive UIs take more time and effort to use, require training, documentation, and lots of technical support, all of which cost money.

- Even captive audiences have more choice than you might think. They might inefficiently delegate tasks to someone else, use alternatives such as making phone calls, or just flat out refuse to use the unintuitive app.

- **People can learn!** *People learn things all the time, so they will just learn how to use our app.* Do you want the success of your app to depend upon people learning stuff? I don't think so. More about this excuse in a moment.

- **Efficiency is more important!** *Our app is all about efficiency—making it intuitive just gets in the way.* This is simply not true—there is little correlation between efficiency and intuitiveness. The key is to remember that intuitive is defined from the point of view of the target users. Even for the most efficient apps that require training, having clear, consistent, meaningful labels, mnemonic keyboard shortcuts, responsive feedback, and forgiveness go a long way. Doing so leads to more efficiency, lower error rates, and less need for training. **It is wrong to assume that highly efficient apps must be unintuitive.**

FIGURE 1-9 What your employees think of your unintuitive line-of-business app.

Tweet This!

- **Not everything can be made intuitive!** *We have so many different types of users that it's impossible to be intuitive for everyone.* While this claim is partially true (as we'll see in Chapter 5), it doesn't justify poor design for interactions that can easily be made intuitive.

- **Just RTFM it! We have more important things to do.** We saw this one earlier, so we already know that it unnecessarily limits our target market and makes our product vulnerable to competition. Which is important too, right?

FIGURE 1-10 Intuitive UIs can save lives.

The top (weak) excuses **7**

The "people can learn" excuse

The *people can learn* claim seems the most reasonable (because it's true!) and possibly the hardest one to refute, so **let's explore it a bit more.**

FIGURE 1-11 The Blackberry Z10.

Mobile design is one of my specialties, so **I have six completely different smartphones to have firsthand experience with their designs and interaction models. The oldest one is a Blackberry Z10.** (In case you aren't familiar, the Z10 was Blackberry's bold attempt to compete with iOS and Android.) I bought it because of its unusual interaction model and innovative design. Let's just say that buying it made sense at the time.

The Z10 doesn't have a Home button, as with iOS, nor does it have Back, Home, and Recents, as with Android. Instead of using standard navigation patterns, most navigation is achieved through edge swipes. I would like to share the story of my purchasing process:

I went to a Verizon store (my carrier in the U.S.) to buy a Blackberry Z10. I thought to ask for a quick demo, so the salesperson started confidently showing me the Z10's various features. At some point, he stopped and said, "You know what? I'm stuck. I'm sorry, I had training on this phone two months ago, but unfortunately, I don't know what to do now."

As it happened, that store couldn't sell me an unlocked phone so I had to buy it from another Verizon store. I thought I would ask for another demo, so the salesperson started confidently showing me the Z10's various features. Guess what happened? At some point, she stopped and said, "I'm stuck. I had training on this phone two months ago, but unfortunately, I don't know what to do now."

Now, let's work this through. Suppose we are Blackberry. We used to own the smartphones market (our products were called "crackberries" because they were so addictive) and we want to get back in the game. **Which design approach makes more sense? The intuitive design that users can pick up and immediately figure out on their own, or the radically innovative design with an unintuitive navigation model that our own salespeople can't even demo?**

I vote for the intuitive design. Yes, it's true that users can learn, but will they? What happens if they don't learn or don't remember what they learned? As we'll see in Chapter 5, not everything can be intuitive and it does make sense to design certain interactions to be strategically unintuitive (instead of accidentally unintuitive), but only if those interactions are advanced, infrequent, and optional. **Do you want the success of your product to rely on people having to learn its essential interactions?**

Yes, a few extremely successful apps, such as Snapchat, have deliberately unintuitive UIs. But most apps that try this approach fail. Their participation trophy is to be the cutting-edge experience that everyone talks about but nobody actually uses.

Tweet This!

Let's look at one more example. **With Windows 8, Microsoft bet that users would learn how to access the Start Menu if its entry point were removed from the desktop. Microsoft lost that very expensive, completely unnecessary bet.**

FIGURE 1-12 How do you get to the Start Menu?

But it's intuitive once you learn it!

The "people can learn" excuse   9

What you need to succeed

OK, you get it now—you understand that modern UIs need to be intuitive and that modern users demand that they are. **Now all you must do is persuade your team to get on board.** No problem.

This chapter has helped you make the case for intuitive UI in general. Beyond that, you will also need to:

- **Make a persuasive case that a UI is not intuitive.** The definition of intuitive UI in Chapter 2, plus the Eight Attributes of Intuitive UI in Chapter 3, will enable you to do this. If an interaction doesn't meet the definition or is missing any important intuitive attributes, you have found a problem.

- **Make a persuasive case that a UI is intuitive.** For this, the Eight Attributes of Intuitive UI and the interaction lifecycle model in Chapter 3 will help.

- **Make a persuasive case that an unintuitive UI doesn't need to be.** For this, the strategically unintuitive concepts and the Levels of Intuitiveness chart in Chapter 5 will help.

- **Make task flows intuitive.** Intuitive task flows require higher level thinking, which is outlined in Chapter 6.

- **Verify that a UI is intuitive through usability and other types of testing.** For this, the testing techniques for specifically measuring intuitiveness that are outlined in Chapter 7 will help.

As you work through the rest of the book, **keep in mind that your ability to do your best work is determined by how well you can persuade your team members, managers, stakeholders, and clients.** Most likely, every design decision you make will require some sort of approval. **Personal opinion is rarely persuasive, and it's easily trumped by business goals or technical issues. This book will give you the tools you need to be persuasive.**

Tweet This!

Summary

You can no longer expect a product to be successful if it requires documentation or training, because your users are motivated to find an alternative solution that doesn't. Requiring documentation or training makes you vulnerable to competition. A new generation of users demand intuitive, easy-to-use products. RTFM doesn't work anymore. The design world has changed!

Exercises

Apply what you have learned in this chapter with these exercises:

1. Find three examples of formerly popular products that you used heavily but no longer use any more. What do you do now instead? Why?
2. Can you think of a product that you now use that is more complex and harder to use than your previous solution?
3. Have you ever abandoned a product because you couldn't figure out how to use it? What couldn't you figure out? How long did you try before giving up?
4. Can you think of a product that you now use that is simpler and easier to use than a powerful, feature-rich legacy product that it replaced? How did you adapt to the missing features and power?
5. When was the last time you read a product's user manual or watched a video tutorial (for something other than assembly or installation)? How about for a mobile app? How did that affect your opinion of the product?
6. Have you ever recommended a product to a friend or relative that requires reading a user manual? (Answer assuming that you like them. ☺)
7. Have you ever given an App Store or Google Play review? If your rating was less than 5 stars, what specifically caused you to withhold stars?
8. Try this thought experiment: Suppose two equally skilled design teams are competing for a project targeted at highly trained professionals. Team A is requested to make the design 90% intuitive for experienced users, whereas Team B is instructed to make the product as powerful as possible, but not worry about making it intuitive because users will need training anyway. Predict what the resulting designs will look like, and which team will prevail. Provide details. (Many design teams, perhaps unknowingly, are in this very situation.)

> **Thanks to this man, airplanes don't crash into mountains anymore**
>
> In the arcane world of aviation terminology, crashes into mountains were called Controlled Flight into Terrain, or CFIT. It was a vexing problem: Basic navigation should have kept pilots from crashing. But the cockpit navigation technology of that era wasn't intuitive and it was too easy to get disoriented, especially at night or in bad weather.
>
> "I was disappointed," [Don] Bateman, now 84, recalled of the day in 1971 when he flew over the remains of Alaska Airlines Flight 1866, which had slammed into a fog-shrouded ridge. "We needed to do better."
>
> That's exactly what Bateman and his small team of engineers at what is now Honeywell International Inc. did. The device presaged today's mobile mapping applications, dramatically reduced what had been by far the worst class of air crashes and made Honeywell billions of dollars.
>
> If a plane was flying toward a mountain, a screen popped up automatically marking the high ground in yellow and red on a map. If pilots didn't respond, it began a series of increasingly dire warnings. Once a collision became almost imminent, a mechanical voice implored, "Terrain, terrain. Pull up! Pull up!" Compared to the earlier system, it was almost foolproof.
>
> Source: *https://www.bloomberg.com/features/2016-bateman-airplane-safety-device/*

CHAPTER 2

The definition of intuitive UI

You can't design it if you can't define it!

Having an intuitive UI is a top goal for most UX design projects, and my clients invariably describe their top goal as making their products more intuitive. From the users' point of view, saying that they find a product's design to be intuitive is among the highest praise possible. "I love this product—it's so intuitive!" is the ultimate customer review.

One small problem: nobody knows what an "intuitive" UI really is. I know this because I routinely ask (when appropriate, of course). If someone were to tell me they love a product because it is intuitive, I respond by saying "Great! But what does that mean?" It's surprising how vague and impractical many of the responses are.

Even highly experienced designers have difficulty giving a meaningful definition. Designers' understanding of intuitive design is intuitive itself: they know an intuitive design when they see one, but they have a difficult time defining intuitive generally, resorting to vague synonyms like *familiar* or *digestible*.

> *Before proceeding: Give it a go!* Please define what you think it means for a UI to be intuitive as specifically as you can.

When designers try to convince their team that a UI is intuitive (or not), such discussions often become battles of personal opinion. "I find the design is intuitive because it uses common design patterns" or "It's similar to the way my favorite app works." **With managers or developers, expect to lose such battles. Their opinions, plus their business goals and technology cards, will usually trump yours.**

Tweet This!

Some popular but unhelpful definitions

Before I present the definition that I recommend, **let's take a quick look at some popular but impractical definitions.** People often say an intuitive UI is

- ***Simple, easy to use, better*** These aren't good definitions because they confuse intuitive UI with completely different design attributes. We know what *simple* means, what *easy to use* means, and what *better* means—and they are different from what we mean by *intuitive*. Still, they are accurate in the sense that when people say a UI is intuitive, they often mean that they like it or think it is better than the alternatives.

- ***Really "dumbed down" so any idiot can get it*** This definition is flat-out wrong. An intuitive UI isn't dumbed down, and we shouldn't assume that our users are stupid. This viewpoint is so wrong that we will explore it in detail later in this chapter.

- ***An "unrealistically high bar" that most UIs can't achieve*** I have heard many people assert that an intuitive UI is some unattainable perfection. This is wrong, of course, because it's possible to design intuitive UIs once you know how. Suggesting that intuitiveness is unattainable is hardly motivating and, simply put, false.

- ***A gap between the design model and the user model*** This definition comes from Don Norman's *The Design of Everyday Things*. Norman asserts that designers effectively have a conversation with their users. It's not a direct conversation—it takes place through the product. *Design models* are designers' intention for how they believe the product should work, whereas *user models* are users' interpretations of how they think that design works. For an intuitive design, these models should be the same. I love the concept, but it is difficult to apply. To do so, you must figure out the design model, the user model, whether there's a gap between the models, whether that gap is important, and what to do about it. That's way too much figuring.

- ***Familiar*** This definition involves assessing whether target users can apply previously learned knowledge to their interaction with the current design. Successfully doing so requires *consistency* with those prior interactions, otherwise users will be misled or confused. While I agree that intuitive UIs need to leverage previous knowledge, this is a secondary consideration and possibly misleading because many familiar designs are often unintuitive. We'll explore problems with defining *intuitive* as merely *familiar* in Chapter 4.

- ***Learnable*** In this case a design has attributes that make it easy to learn. However, an intuitive UI isn't about making a UI easy to learn—it's about avoiding the need for learning in the first place. We'll explore this distinction in Chapter 4.

- ***Obvious always wins*** I like this one—if it were only obvious what *obvious* means and how to correctly choose the winner.

- ***Whatever Apple does*** As a company, Apple certainly has a high bar for design and an enviable track record for great user experiences (ignoring iTunes). Still, just because Apple does something doesn't make it intuitive. I keep track of all the unintuitive UI I find on my iPhone—it's a very long list.

- ***Not sure, but I know it when I see it—it just feels right*** Although a frequent response to my request for a definition, this answer is an evasion and I suspect a less embarrassing way to say *I have no idea*. You can't design for something—or even recognize if you have it—without being able to define it.

As you can see, there is a lot of confusion.

The lack of a common, practical definition for *intuitive UI* is sometimes used by UX design thought leaders as a reason to dismiss the concept entirely. *Nobody knows what* intuitive *means, so why bother? Let's focus on other design objectives instead.* Let's not repeat their mistake or wallow in their remorse. As designers we need this concept—badly!

We need a better, more specific, more practical definition. So let's define *intuitive UI*!

A practical definition

Here's the definition I find actually useful:

> *A user interface is intuitive when target users understand its behavior and effect without use of reason, memorization, experimentation, assistance, or training.*

Or to rephrase more simply: an intuitive UI is immediately self-explanatory to its target user. Users shouldn't have to think or experiment to figure out what things mean or what just happened.

This is a practical definition because it is focused on the outcome we want. **If your target users must resort to reason, memorizing, experimenting, seeking help, or training, your UI isn't intuitive by definition.** (Remember watching YouTube videos counts as training.)

Tweet This!

If you find this definition narrow, that is very much deliberate. Remember the problem we are trying to solve: few people know what this important UX concept means. An overly broad definition—one that is essentially a synonym for *good*—would fail to address the problem.

The need for a user manual is a clear sign that a UI is not intuitive. In fact, the typical user manual merely explains a product's unintuitive UI in a sensible manner. When I engage with new clients, I ask to review their user manual for this very reason.

FIGURE 2-1 The need for a user manual is a clear sign of an unintuitive UI.

That said, having an unintuitive UI—one that requires experimentation, documentation, and training—doesn't necessarily mean that a product is poorly designed. Such a product might be usable for highly motivated, well-trained users. **Many successful products have unintuitive UIs—sometimes deliberately—as you'll see in Chapter 5.**

But as we explored in Chapter 1, **users' expectations are rapidly rising and the next generation of users don't want to take the time and effort to learn unintuitive UIs.** Requiring documentation and training limits your market. If your legacy product has a lot of unintuitive UI, you are now at a significant competitive disadvantage.

If you are an experienced designer, there's a good chance that your own definition of *intuitive* is different—perhaps completely different. That's not a problem in practice, as long as applying that definition results in good design decisions and productive discussions with your team. If not, consider upgrading.

Not the dictionary definition

Before proceeding, I should mention that you won't find this definition of intuitive UI in any dictionary. **The typical dictionary states that *intuitive* means *instinctive*—in other words, behavior and knowledge that we are born with.** But that's not helpful with respect to intuitive UI.

Our definition of intuitive UI, as well as the Eight Attributes of Intuitive UI defined in Chapter 3, are all relative to a product's *target users*. What matters is whether we can realistically expect the target users to know or do something based on the knowledge they already have and the context they are in. **When they learned that knowledge—whether at birth or five minutes ago—hardly matters.** In other words, a UI can be intuitive to one set of users but not to another, because of their different backgrounds, contexts, and knowledge. (But, that said, in practice I find that most unintuitive UIs are unintuitive for everybody.)

The manifestation of intuitive UI

Designers often refer to well-designed interactions as being *smooth*. As you might guess, I avoid using vague, abstract words like *smooth*, but we can try to redeem it with a specific definition.
An interaction is smooth when

- Users complete a task successfully on the first try.
- Users make very few mistakes along the way.
- Users maintain their flow, without awkward pauses to think things through or experiment.

By contrast, an interaction isn't smooth when users have to experiment because mistakes are essentially interaction experiments. This leads to what I call the *Manifestation of Intuitive UI*:

> *You can observe that a UI is intuitive when users successfully complete tasks on the first try consistently, without making mistakes.*
>
> Tweet This!

This is what intuitive UI looks like, and it's observable and measurable. Yes, it's a thing!

Is this intuitive?

Let's give this definition of intuitive UI a go by looking at some example designs. Admittedly, it's far easier to determine whether a UI is unintuitive by definition than to determine whether one is intuitive, so the following examples all have problems. (But don't worry, you will soon be able to figure out whether a UI is intuitive by using the Eight Attributes of Intuitive UI, described in Chapter 3.)

For each of these designs, apply the details of the definition—is reason, memorization, experimentation, assistance, or training required?—to describe its problems. In each case, I provide the task or context to get you started.

Example 1:

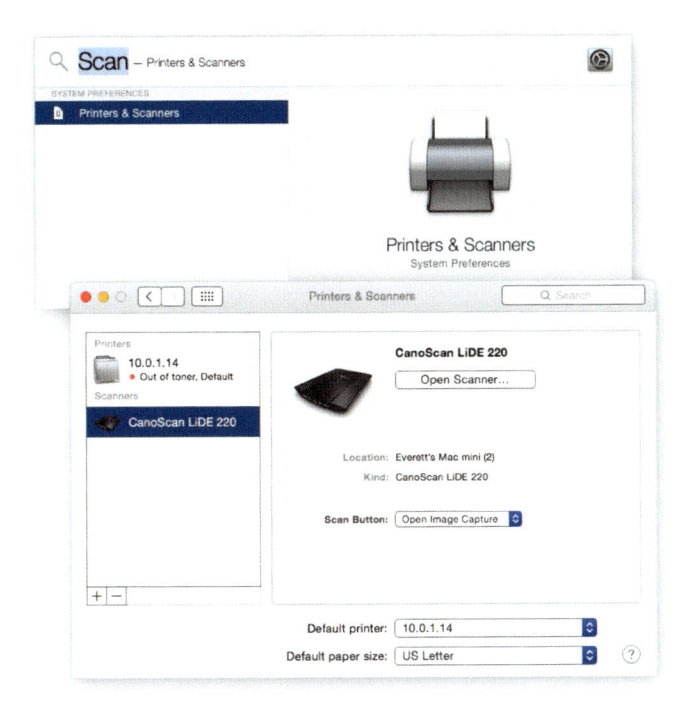

You need to scan a document and are looking for an app to help you do it.

Is this intuitive?   **17**

Example 2:

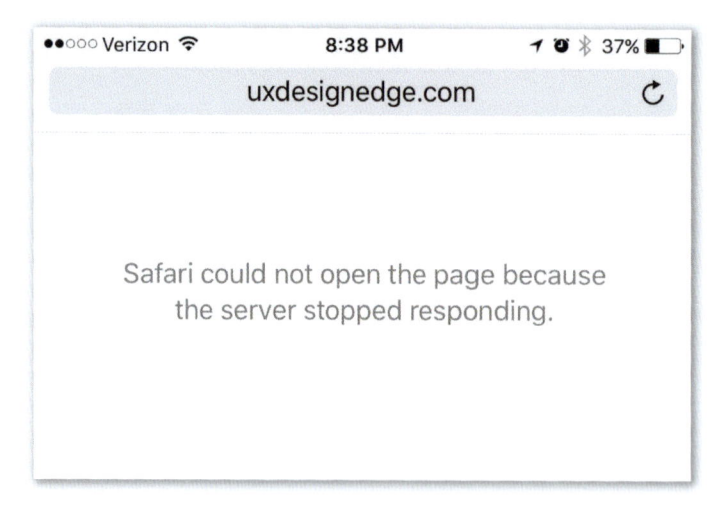

> ••○○○ Verizon 🌐　　8:38 PM　　✈ 🕐 ✱ 37%🔋
>
> uxdesignedge.com　↻
>
> Safari could not open the page because the server stopped responding.

You're connected to Wi-Fi, yet email and other apps don't work. What's the problem?

Example 3:

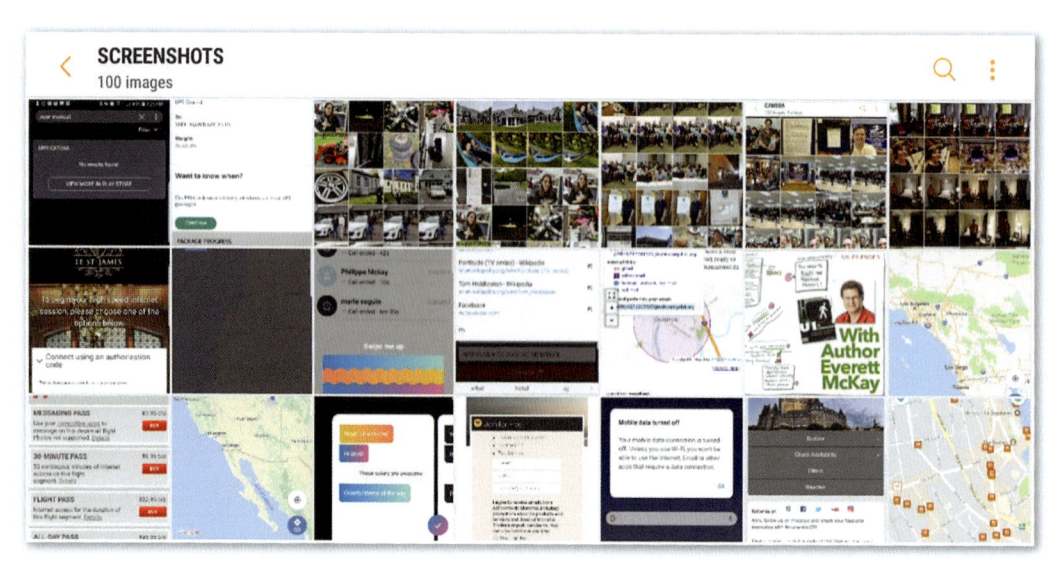

For this photo selection UI, how do you select multiple photos?

Example 4:

For this security control panel, how do you set the time?

Were you able to describe the problems? Compare your results to mine at the end of the chapter.

Intuitive UIs are not dumbed down

I mentioned that occasionally people define intuitive as *dumbed down*. This is not only wrong and disrespectful to our users but also counterproductive.

It is not uncommon for a team with a poorly designed product that users dislike to attempt to fix it with a severely dumbed-down, spoon-fed, irritating design. Teams that try this invariably discover that their users prefer the original—even if it's unintuitive. Such stories are not an indictment of intuitive UI but of dumbed-down UI. Dumbing down says that you believe your users are dumb—which you should never do!

Of course, different target users have different ranges of technology and domain skills, as well as different language skills. Not everyone is an expert, and it's a common mistake to assume that our target users have the same knowledge that we do. If many of your target users aren't native English speakers, you should adjust the UI text to an appropriate reading level. **But these are normal user-centered design factors, not making dumbing down a goal.**

Tweet This! **Assume your users are smart but very busy. They aren't expert users, and they lack the time and motivation to figure out how your app works.** They know their goals but not necessarily the details of how to achieve them. They probably (almost certainly?) didn't read the app's documentation, so they know only what your app tells them in the context they are in. **It's often the case that your users know their domain much better than you do, but of course they don't know how your app works nearly as well as you. After all, they didn't design it—you did!**

To give you a framework, let me present a user sophistication spectrum:

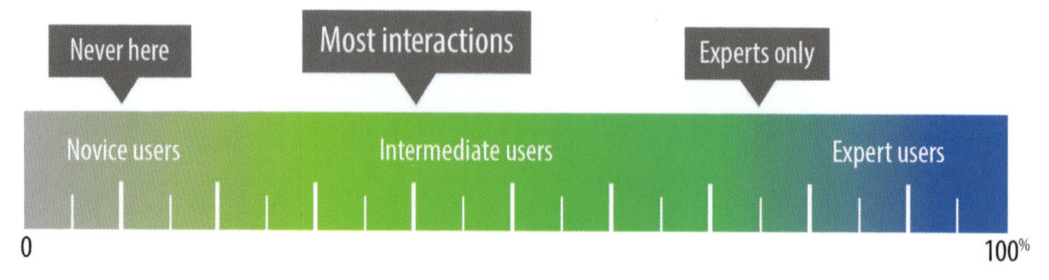

FIGURE 2-2 *The user sophistication spectrum. Most interactions should target intermediate users.*

Most interactions should be designed for intermediate users, with a bias towards smart users who are in a hurry. Interactions that require experience, memorization, and perhaps training should be biased towards low experts—not super experts. Unless you have a very specialized product, assume that super experts are rare and are satisfied by well-designed interactions targeted at low experts.

Design most interactions for intermediate users, with a bias towards smart users who are in a hurry. Assume your users are smart but that super experts are rare.

Summary

Remember the definition of intuitive UI and get in the habit of applying it. (It's a good idea to get your team on board first.) You will be surprised how useful it is. **After all, if your target users need to think through or reason out your UI, memorize, experiment, consult the user manual, ask someone for help, or get training, your app isn't intuitive by definition.**

Exercises

Apply what you have learned in this chapter with the following exercises:

1. Find an example UI that you believe is unintuitive. Try to convince someone else that it is unintuitive based on the definition of intuitive UI you learned in this chapter. Were you able to make your case?

2. Find an example UI that you believe is unintuitive because it requires reasoning. Repeat for experimentation, memorization, documentation, and training. Do you find applying the definition helpful when assessing designs?

3. Find an example UI that requires experimentation to use (and consider *trial and error* to be experimentation). Redesign it to not require experimentation. Is your redesign better? Is it now intuitive?

4. Design an intuitive way to set the clock for a car radio. To evaluate intuitiveness, users should be able to set the current time correctly without making any mistakes. (Mistakes reveal the need to reason, experiment, and memorize.) Test your design by having people set the time, and expect to do several iterations of your design to get it right. What did you change in those iterations and what was the effect of each change?

5. Car manufactures strive to keep instrumentation as simple as possible. Repeat the previous exercise, but try to simplify your design as much as you can, including removing buttons. Determine which simplifications result in making the design unintuitive.

6. Purposely design an everyday control like a light switch or a power button to be unintuitive. Explain why the design is unintuitive based on the definition of intuitive UI.

7. Find two apps that enable users to perform similar tasks but one that you think is intuitive and one that is not. Can you find reasons why users might prefer the unintuitive app? Do you think this preference might change over time?

8. Is driving a car intuitive? Try to make the case both ways. Which case is more compelling?

My answers

EXAMPLE 1: Even though the Mac OSX Spotlight feature gives the correct match, it doesn't look like the correct match. You are looking for a scanner app not the Printers and Scanners Preferences, so there is a good chance you will keep looking, requiring both reason and experimentation.

EXAMPLE 2: Even though you are connected to a Wi-Fi hotspot with a strong signal and the status icon indicates that all is well, you need to pull up a web page in a browser and either sign in, provide your name, or accept the terms and conditions. While some Wi-Fi hotspots do this automatically, many don't, requiring reason, memorization, and experimentation.

EXAMPLE 3: This photo selection UI lacks a multiple-selection *affordance* (defined in Chapter 3) that indicates multiple selection is possible. Consequently, advanced users might experiment to determine whether multiple selection is supported (and it is, through long press). Novice users would require experimentation or training or, more likely, would select a single file at a time.

EXAMPLE 4: The security control panel has dozens of functions, but only Off, Away, and the three emergency button pairs are self-explanatory. Everything else requires consulting the documentation and possibly memorization, even setting the time. It appears the designers of this control panel assumed that their users were trained technicians or people who don't mind looking up routine tasks in a user manual. As a homeowner, I can state with confidence that their assumption is wrong.

CHAPTER 3

The Eight Attributes of Intuitive UI

How do I design intuitive UI? Let me count the ways.

In Chapter 2, you learned a practical definition of intuitive UI. **The definition helps us determine whether a design is intuitive, but alone it doesn't give us the insight we need to make a design intuitive in the first place. For that, we need the Eight Attributes of Intuitive UI.**

> **Reading tip: This chapter is much longer than the others because it explores the details required to make designs intuitive. If you're pressed for time, consider the details in the eight intuitive attributes sections to be reference material that you can return to as needed.**

The interaction lifecycle

How can we determine these intuitive attributes? Performing extensive usability studies and analyzing the design problems found for trends would be one approach—and this was the one used by Jakob Nielsen and Rolf Molich to derive their *Usability Heuristics*.

However, I prefer a more goal-driven, principled approach: analyzing the sequence of steps—both mental and physical—that a user performs to complete a task with your app, identifying the potential problems for each step, and determining design attributes that prevent those problems. **I call the sequence of steps the *interaction lifecycle*. If the user can get through all the steps and successfully complete the task without reasoning, experimentation, memorization, documentation, or training, then our definition of intuitive UI has been met.** By contrast, if the user can't complete all the steps of the interaction lifecycle, that meets our definition of unintuitive.

Here is the interaction lifecycle. To interact with your product, the user

1. Sets a goal to accomplish.
2. Finds the starting point that might achieve the goal.
3. Performs the action.
4. Observes the action's results to determine whether the goal was achieved as expected.
5. If successful, continues to the next goal; otherwise, fixes any problems and tries again.

What could go wrong during this interaction lifecycle? Plenty, it turns out. Here are potential problems for each step:

1. The user isn't sure what to do next.
2. The user can't find the starting point or mistakenly chooses the wrong starting point.
3. The user makes a mistake performing the action—provides incorrect input or makes a poor decision. Perhaps the user doesn't understand the action or finds the action error-prone.
4. The user doesn't observe the results, doesn't observe them in a timely manner, or is misled by the feedback or results of the action.
5. If there is a problem, there is no error feedback or the user doesn't understand what to do about it. To fix the problem, the motivated user is extremely inconvenienced—often having to start the interaction completely over. (By contrast, the unmotivated user might just give up.)

Let's now identify the design attributes that prevent or mitigate these problems.

The Eight Attributes of Intuitive UI

And now the moment you have been waiting for: **the Eight Attributes of Intuitive UI are discoverability, affordance, comprehensibility, responsive feedback, predictability, efficiency, forgiveness, and explorability.** The following poster helps you visualize how these attributes flow through the interaction lifecycle.

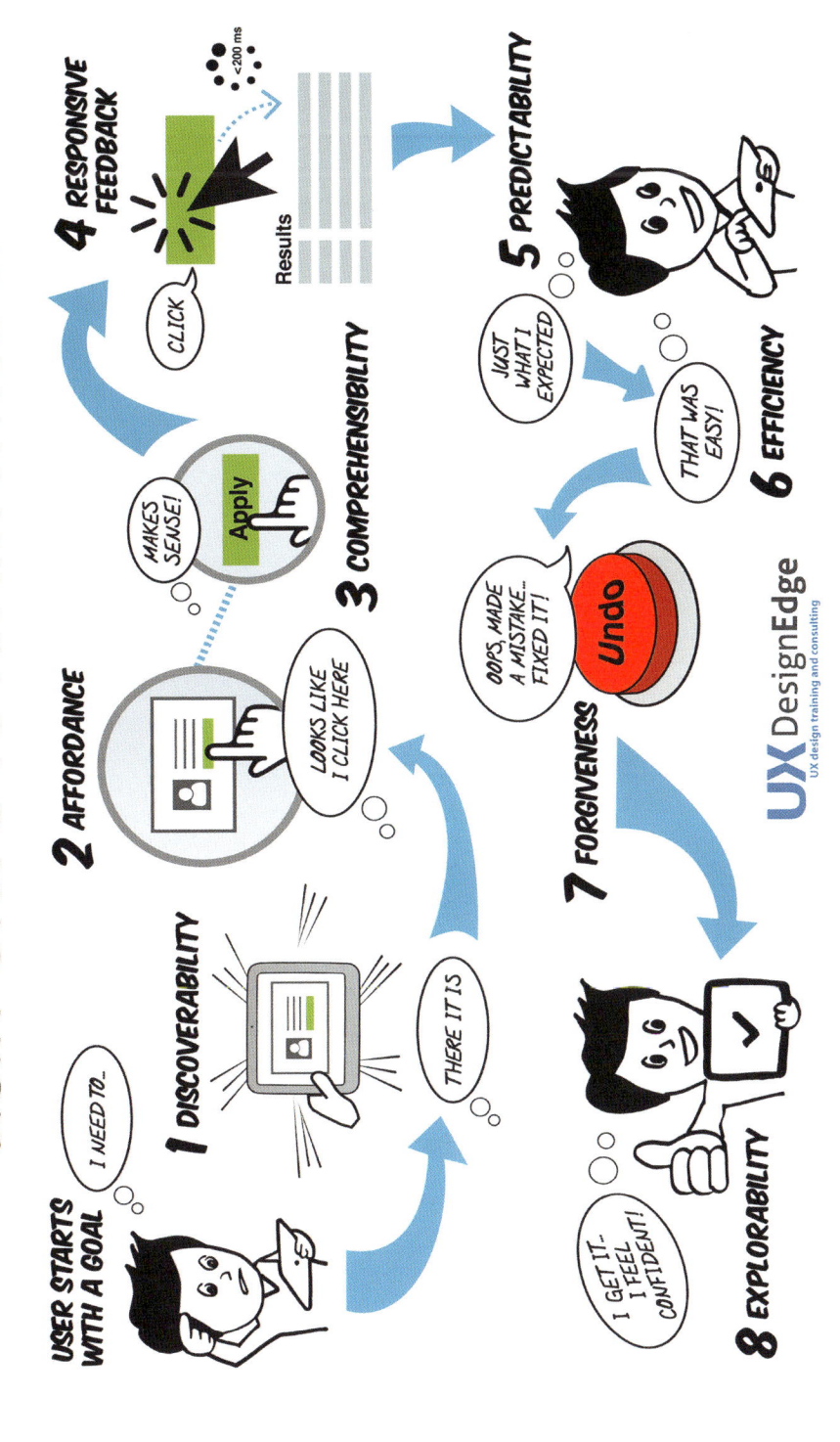

FIGURE 3-1 The Eight Attributes of Intuitive UI.

The Eight Attributes of Intuitive UI 25

Let's look at each attribute in detail, but first, here's how they map to the interaction lifecycle steps:

1. Sets a goal to accomplish.
2. Finds the starting point that might achieve the goal. **Discoverability, affordance, comprehensibility, predictability.**
3. Performs the action specific to the goal. **Affordance, efficiency, explorability.**
4. Observes the action's results to determine whether goal was achieved as expected. **Responsive feedback, predictability.**
5. If successful, continues to the next goal; otherwise, fixes any problems. **Forgiveness, comprehensibility.**

Note that there is some overlap of attributes between the interaction lifecycle steps. For example, with Step 2, to find the starting point, users must first find the right UI element physically (*discoverability*), determine that it is interactive (*affordance*), understand its label to confirm that it's what they are looking for (*comprehensibility*), and accurately determine that its result will meet expectations (*predictability*). And three of these attributes in Step 2 also serve other steps in the interaction lifecycle.

The five steps of the interaction lifecycle help us understand how users interact with a UI, and we need to confirm that we have the right attributes for each step of their interaction. Now that we have done this, **let's put the interaction lifecycle aside and focus on the Eight Attributes of Intuitive UI.**

Using the interaction lifecycle helps us determine the attributes required to complete an interaction in a way that satisfies our definition of intuitive UI.

Discoverability

***Discoverability* is the target users' ability to locate the UI elements needed to achieve a goal—when they need them.**
Because discoverability facilitates the first step in the interaction lifecycle, it is crucial for intuitive interactions. If users can't find what they are looking for, none of the other intuitive attributes matter.

Discoverability helps users find the features they need to achieve their goals—when they need them.

It's much easier to characterize what isn't discoverable than what is, so let's tackle discoverability by identifying common design mistakes that harm discoverability. It turns out there are several.

Provide an obvious starting point

Frequent tasks need a clear, visually obvious starting point.
Users need to know where to look (and possibly interact) first for common tasks. Advanced, infrequent tasks can be much less obvious.

FIGURE 3-2 The original Windows 95 Start Menu gave users a clear, visually obvious starting point for frequent tasks.

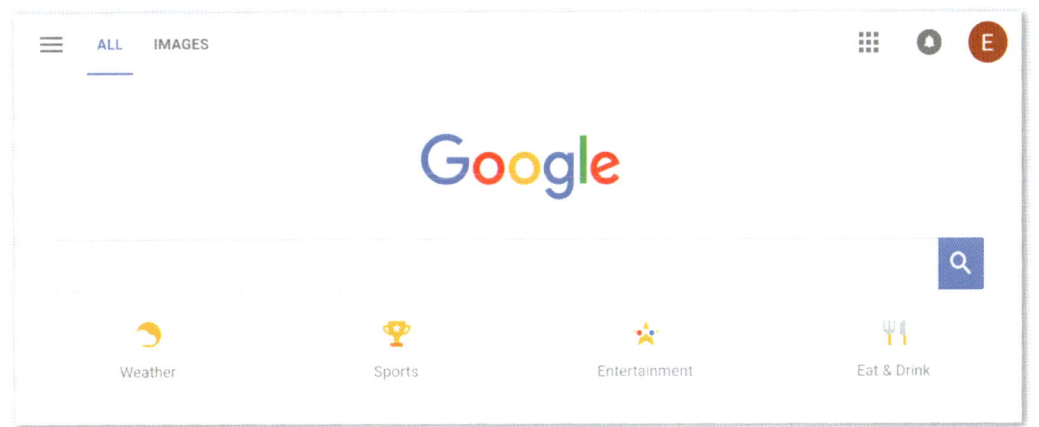

FIGURE 3-3 Google's famously ultra-simple home page makes it visually obvious what it does and how to get started.

Discoverability — Provide an obvious starting point 27

Often users need to interact with a specific object. **The best place to present object-specific commands is directly on the object itself, either persistently or by entering an edit mode.**

A common pattern for poor discoverability is an initial, empty state—especially for lists, collections, or initial configurations. Common solutions are to provide initial samples (such as sample photos in a photo album) or provide clear instructions on how to add items. Doing so is a form of user onboarding, which strives to get new users familiar and successful with an app as quickly as possible.

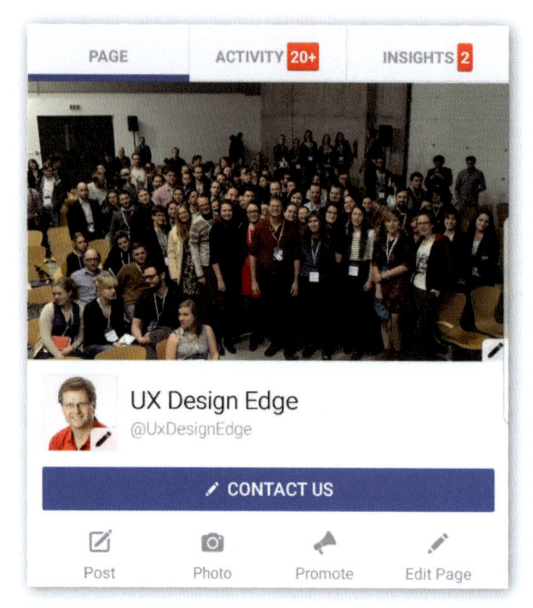

FIGURE 3-4 If you own a page, Facebook allows you to enter edit mode through tapping an object.

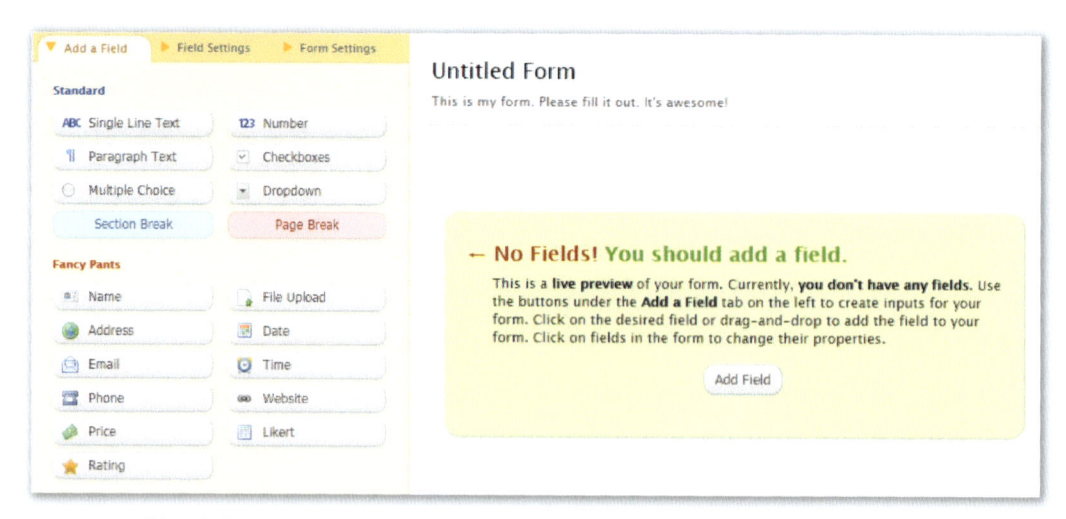

FIGURE 3-5 When building a form, Wufoo improves discoverability by explicitly indicating how to add the first item.

28   Chapter 3   The Eight Attributes of Intuitive UI

Unintuitive: Poor presentation

An interactive UI element has a poor presentation when it doesn't look interactive—or possibly doesn't look interactive *now*. This could be due to missing affordance (the second intuitive attribute), nonobvious dynamic affordance (revealed on hover or another interaction but not appearing interactive now), appearing disabled, or being so small or hard to find that users don't notice it. Such examples of poor presentation greatly diminish a UI element's discoverability.

FIGURE 3-6 There's a reason for Trello encouraging users to drag the link to bookmarks—links don't have a drag affordance!

Unintuitive: Poor location and layout

An interactive UI element has a poor location by context, layout, or convention. For context, users expect proximity and sensible physical layout. For a given UI element, users expect any relevant commands will be physically near that element. The pairing of labels to their associated UI elements should never be ambiguous. They also expect the reverse—that any commands physically near the element are relevant to that object unless there is a clear separator. A classic unintuitive example is a DVD player with the On/Off switch next to the DVD tray and the button for ejecting discs in a completely different place.

FIGURE 3-7 Users naturally assume the button nearest the DVD tray (on the far left) would be Open/Close, but it's actually On/Off. The Open/Close button? The button on the far right—furthest away from the DVD tray.

Tweet This!

A goal of well-designed layout is to suggest relationships. Group boxes (along with panes) are often used to make relationships explicit, whereas separators are used to make the lack of relationship explicit. Generally, it's better to show relationships using layout alone and resort to panes, boxes, and separators only when necessary.

Regarding convention, users learn where to expect certain types of commands, and placing them elsewhere might harm discoverability. Primary commands are often large and placed directly in the immediate context. By contrast, secondary commands might be found in a contextual menu or perhaps a hamburger menu. Important, frequently used, general commands are usually directly in the header, whereas less frequently used, meta commands are often in the footer.

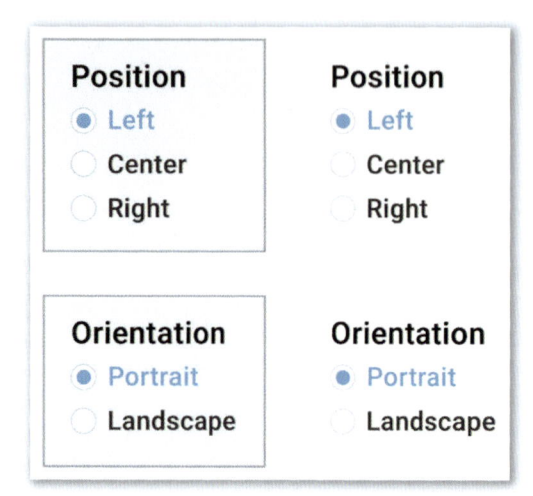

FIGURE 3-8 Using layout, along with group boxes and separators, to show relationships. But avoid the group boxes unless you really need them.

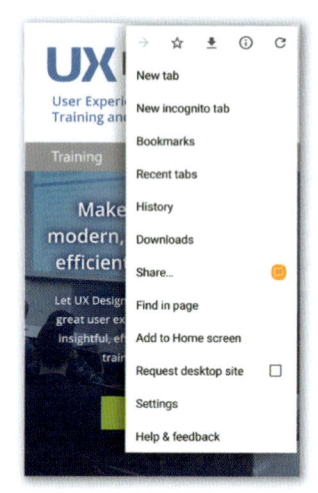

FIGURE 3-9 Hamburger menus (and their kabab variants) are an excellent place for secondary commands but a poor place for primary commands. When possible, put primary commands in the immediate context instead.

Finally, it's worth mentioning that a top cause of user frustration is when designers decide to move UI elements from one release to the next, even if the new location makes more sense (to new users) than the old one. **Be strategic when placing or moving UI elements across releases; make sure new locations are worth any frustration to your current users.**

Tweet This!

Unintuitive: Poor recognition

Users might find the desired UI element immediately but not recognize it as such and keep looking. (Perhaps they'll eventually return to the element after applying the process of elimination to the remaining elements on the page, but this reveals a discoverability problem.) This could be due to poor comprehensibility (the third intuitive attribute), along with labels that are overly

Chapter 3   The Eight Attributes of Intuitive UI

specific (making users decide that what they're looking for isn't there) or overly vague (making users decide that a more specific and appropriate element must be elsewhere).

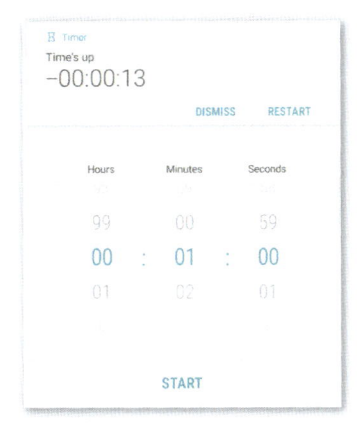

FIGURE 3-10 Have you ever noticed how difficult it can be to turn off an alarm or timer? The dismiss or stop button is often presented as a secondary command, making it easy to tap the more prominent command accidentally — as if starting another timer or snoozing were the far more likely intention.

Unintuitive: Too many competing options

Perhaps the desired UI element is hidden in plain sight but users can't find it because they are overwhelmed by all the options. It's like playing *Where's Waldo?* Programmers are especially fond of designing overly complex, jam-packed screens in the mistaken belief that doing so results in a more efficient UI. This approach fails because there's a limit to how much users can discover and comprehend simultaneously. Better to take advantage of priority, context, and grouping to make things easier to find.

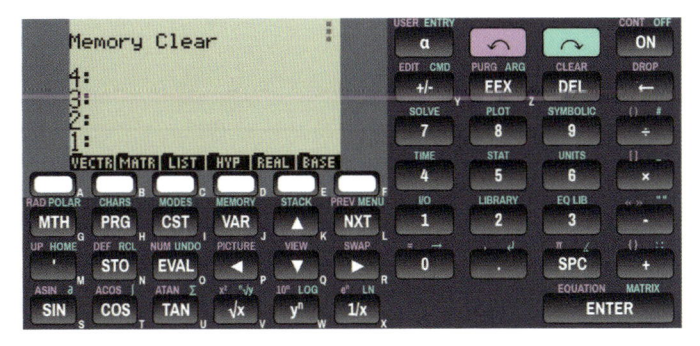

FIGURE 3-11 Complex physical UIs might need this style of presentation, but modern dynamic UIs don't.

Discoverability — Unintuitive: Too many competing options   31

Unintuitive: Just plain hard to find, like a puzzle

The desired UI elements are hidden initially, then revealed dynamically when users perform some action. Such interactions feel like a puzzle, as if you are trying to access a jewelry box's secret compartment. Some users never find these UI elements and their interaction with your product fails.

FIGURE 3-12 Unintuitive dynamic UI often feels like accessing a secret compartment.

FIGURE 3-13 Design static UI so that users can accurately predict any dynamic UI. Here, a long press reveals the ability to drag items to your wish list, but there's no way to predict this from the static UI.

Here is the dynamic UI challenge: on one hand, we don't want the overall experience to feel overwhelming, but on the other hand, we don't want it to feel like a puzzle either. The trick to get the right balance. Display enough information statically so that users can confidently and accurately predict (the fifth attribute) what they will see dynamically. **When designing dynamic interactions, assume that users won't proceed if they lack confidence.**

Tweet This!

> ### Best additional ways to evaluate discoverability
>
> In addition to usability studies, eye-tracking studies are an excellent tool for evaluating discoverability generally and recognition problems specifically. It's fascinating to observe users finding what they're looking for immediately, only to continue looking because they didn't realize it. Users need confidence before they tap something—unless they are so desperate that they abandon all hope and start tapping everything to solve your UI puzzle.

32   Chapter 3   The Eight Attributes of Intuitive UI

2 AFFORDANCE

Affordance

An *affordance* is a visual property of a UI element that suggests, first, that the element is interactive and, second, how to interact with it. Once affordances have helped users determine that a UI element is interactive, they should further help users understand how to perform its primary interaction (such as tap) and, on rare occasions, secondary interactions (such as long press or 3D Touches). For an intuitive UI, users shouldn't have to reason, experiment, or memorize to determine that a UI element is interactive and enabled—or how to interact with it.

Affordances are the visual properties of a UI element that suggest how to perform an interaction.

Affordances are often a visual metaphor of some real-world counterpart: buttons, radio buttons, sliders, knobs, spinners, handles, grabbers, and slide-out trays are all based on real-world interactions.

The most basic affordance is a button, which visually suggests clicking or tapping. By convention, colored or underlined text is assumed to be a link, which also visually suggests clicking or tapping, although the link affordance is less obvious and potentially misleading when compared to a button.

FIGURE 3-14 Highlighting interactive controls on tap or hover makes their affordances more obvious. In this example, the search command is highlighted on tap.

FIGURE 3-15 The flashing caret clearly affords the ability to type into this text box. Just one problem: the window isn't active, so the flashing caret is completely misleading.

Consistency is crucial here—if an element looks interactive, make sure it is. If it looks like a button or link, make sure it is. Putting text in a box creates the appearance of a button and misleads the user. To emphasize some text, make it bold or italicized rather than underlined.

FIGURE 3-16 For this GPS, guess where you are supposed to tap to enter the address. Not the address fields, as you would expect, but their labels.

There are other affordances. The following table shows the most common affordances, along with their meaning—starting with plain text as a baseline. Again, don't use these affordances unless the UI element has the associated behavior.

AFFORDANCE	MEANING	SAMPLE
Plain text	Ordinary UI text, such as a label or an instruction.	8 Steps to Intuitive UI
Interaction instruction	Ordinary UI text instruction. Avoid except for unexpected secondary interactions.	8 Steps to Intuitive UI Slide for more
Button frame	Indicates that the element is clickable or tappable.	8 Steps to Intuitive UI
Link	Indicates that the element is clickable. Shown with normal-sized colored text. Maybe underlined, but an underline isn't necessary if the text is obviously a link from the context. Hovering changes pointer to a hand to confirm that the text is a link.	8 Steps to Intuitive UI
Edit box	Indicates that the text is editable. The box appearance might be subtle until the user clicks or taps it. Clicking displays a flashing caret to indicate where the interaction will take place.	8 Steps to Intuitive UI
Drop-down arrow	Indicates that a drop-down menu will be displayed where the arrow points.	8 Steps to Intuitive UI

34 Chapter 3 The Eight Attributes of Intuitive UI

AFFORDANCE	MEANING	SAMPLE
Scroll arrows	Indicates that a list or other content is scrollable in the direction of the arrow. Always used in pairs.	Intuitive / Discoverable / Affordance
Chevron	Indicates that any remaining items will be shown (or hidden) where the chevron points. For iOS, a right-pointing chevron indicates that selection will advance to another screen. For Android, a left-pointing chevron in the upper-left corner of the screen (known as Up) indicates moving up in the navigation hierarchy.	8 Steps to Intuitive UI >
Colored background or frame	Indicates that the item has been selected.	Intuitive / Discoverable / Affordance • Eight Steps | Intuitive UI
Check	Indicates that the item has been selected.	✔ 8 Steps to Intuitive UI
Check box	Indicates that the item is independently selectable.	☑ 8 Steps to Intuitive UI
Switch	Indicates that the item is independently selectable. An accessible, touch-friendly check box.	🟢 8 Steps to Intuitive UI
Option circle	Indicates that the item is a mutually exclusive selection.	⦿ 8 Steps ○ Intuitive UI
Open/Close	Indicates that the item is a container that can be expanded or collapsed.	[+] 8 Steps to Intuitive UI [−] 8 Steps to Intuitive UI
Handles	Indicates that the object can be moved, resized, and partially selected.	8 Steps to Intuitive UI www.uxdesignreviews.com
Grabber	Indicates that a surface can be slid.	8 Steps to Intuitive UI
Separator	Adding a line shows separation, often to add more functionality. For example, adding a line to a setting indicates tapping will reveal advanced settings.	8 Steps to Intuitive UI ⌄ 8 Steps to Intuitive UI 🟢
Bold text	Indicates that the UI element is important but doesn't change its interaction.	**8 Steps to Intuitive UI**

Affordance – Introduction   35

AFFORDANCE	MEANING	SAMPLE
Light gray text	Indicates that the UI element is disabled.	8 Steps to Intuitive UI
Flashing	Rapid flashing indicates that the user must respond immediately. Slow flashing (pulsing) attracts attention but doesn't demand attention or a response.	8 Steps to Intuitive UI
X	Indicates that a window or pane can be closed or that the associated object or text will be deleted.	8 Steps to Intuitive UI

Currently, the trend is toward minimal, subtle affordances. For example, Android material design uses input lines instead of complete boxes for text input.

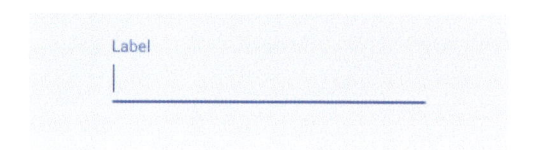

FIGURE 3-17 An input line is a subtle affordance for an edit box.

That said, make sure that the affordance is obvious—which might not be the case if it is placed too far away from the user's attention.

FIGURE 3-18 The top UI element looks like a noninteractive banner—until you see the drop-down arrow at the far right. Placing the drop-down arrow next to the label solves this problem.

Obvious always wins

You would think the need for clear, unambiguous affordances would be obvious, but on occasion designers try to eliminate them—only to end up regretting it. A famous example is when Microsoft temporarily removed the Start Menu button from the Windows 8 desktop. Where did access to the Start Menu go? How did you get back to the desktop from the Start Menu? Nobody knew—highly experienced users no longer knew how the product worked. As Luke Wroblewski, an internationally recognized digital product leader, likes to say, *obvious always wins*.

There was a time when designers removed affordances to eliminate skeuomorphism. *Skeuomorphism* is when designs include decorative real-world elements that aren't necessary for the interaction. For example, an address book might have a leather binding (with folds!), stitching, and dog-eared page corners. Such design elements aren't necessary and are merely decorative. Actual affordances are definitely necessary and should not be considered skeuomorphic.

FIGURE 3-19 The original Mac OS X Address Book applet had many skeuomorphic decorative design elements. While there is no need for decorations like stitching, the buttons need to look interactive.

The need for labels

In *The Design of Everyday Things*, Don Norman famously points out how door handles have affordances. For example, some handles indicate pulling whereas others indicate pushing. If the affordance is misleading, the design flaw is often fixed with a label. I'm sure you've had the experience: you try to open a door, so you pull, pull, pull, until finally you see the label that says *Push*. **As a result, Norman concludes, "If a door handle needs a sign, its design is probably faulty."**

Unintuitive

FIGURE 3-20 Are you supposed to pull or push this door? The affordance clearly indicates pull, but the label says otherwise. These are known as Norman doors.

Affordance – The need for labels 37

The Design of Everyday Things is a well-named book, because it is about everyday things and not technology. Here is my translation of Norman's insight for intuitive UI:

If a UI element needs a label to explain its interaction, its affordance has failed.

Of course, many UI elements need labels, but those labels should focus on the purpose of the element—not on how to do the primary interaction. Having to explain a UI element's primary interaction in a label clearly indicates that its affordance isn't working. Apply this principle to figure out the problem in Example 1 in the "Is this intuitive?" section near the end of this chapter.

That said, I refer to *primary* interactions here for a reason—affordances often don't indicate secondary interactions, such as long presses, 3D Touches, right-clicks, or even direct manipulation like swipes. This isn't a problem if these secondary interactions are targeted at advanced users for optional interactions. If these secondary interactions are intended as fundamental or important interactions for nonexperts, however, there's definitely a problem. While it might be better to give important secondary interactions a clear affordance, consider using a label or coach mark for this purpose.

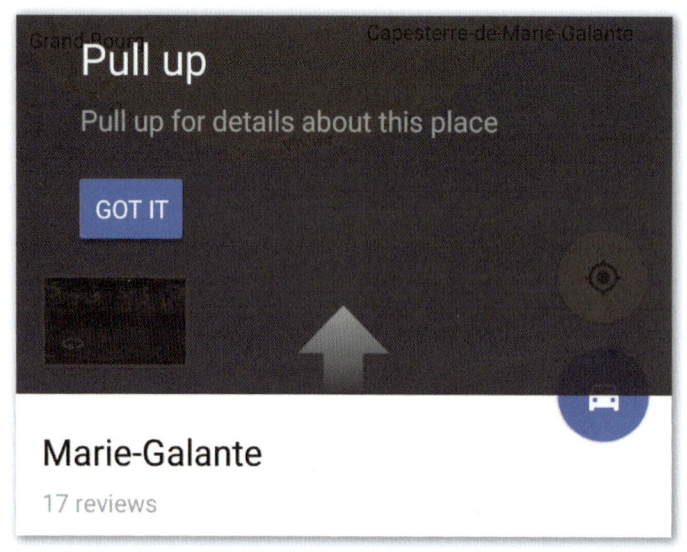

FIGURE 3-21 This coach mark indicates that the swipe gesture reveals more information. Adding a grabber affordance would eliminate the need for the coach mark.

38   Chapter 3   The Eight Attributes of Intuitive UI

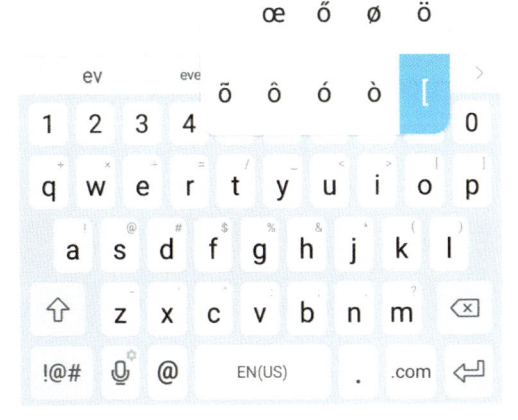

FIGURE 3-22 The key labels and their superscripts indicate both the secondary interaction of long press and what to expect (the result) when you do it.

> ### Best additional ways to evaluate affordance
>
> In addition to usability studies, click testing is a great way to find affordance problems. With a click test, you present a static image of a UI and ask users where they would click to perform a specific task. Success requires users to identify the correct interactive elements without experimenting (which includes hovering).
>
> You can also perform targeted design reviews to find affordance problems. These reviews should help you make sure that all commonly used commands have a clear affordance. Labels that explain an interaction are a sign of an affordance problem. Note that advanced, infrequent, or optional interactions (like shortcuts and gestures) don't always need an affordance, as we'll see in Chapter 5.

Affordance – The need for labels

3 COMPREHENSIBILITY

Comprehensibility

***Comprehensibility* is the target user's ability to understand the meaning and effect of a UI element**—enough to recognize that it is the right element for the desired task, to understand what the element does, and to make the right choices while interacting with it.

Comprehensibility is the user's ability to understand the meaning and effect of a UI element.

Doing so requires users to understand the meaning of labels (either text or icon) or instructions and to make an informed decision based on expected prior knowledge and current context. In practice, comprehensibility often boils down to speaking the target user's language, meeting their expectations, using appropriate icons, making labels self-explanatory, and asking questions that target users know how to answer.

Speaking the target user's language

Tweet This!

Speaking the user's language is a requirement. Make the UI text a concise version of what you'd actually say to the target user in person. If the text is completely unlike what you would say in person, rephrase it. Consider this example:

☑ Print on both sides   ☑ Duplex printing

FIGURE 3-23 Which of these would you say in person: "Would you like to print on both sides of the paper?" or "Would you like duplex printing?"

Comprehensibility is what matters here—much more than technical accuracy. Given a choice between a technically inaccurate label or icon that your target users understand and a technically accurate one that isn't well understood, choose the comprehensible alternative.

FIGURE 3-24 Of these five glyphs, which is the best choice to indicate Network for nontechnical users? It's the Wi-Fi icon (on the far right), even though it's technically inaccurate because it excludes wired connections.

Chapter 3   The Eight Attributes of Intuitive UI

It's a common guideline to avoid jargon, but a much better guideline is to avoid *unnecessary* jargon. Jargon is a special language used by particular groups to communicate effectively, so it's not a problem if your target users are members of that group. In addition to unnecessary jargon, **you should also avoid *unnecessary* acronyms and abbreviations, which are unfortunately all too common.**

Here are some additional considerations to make sure you are speaking the user's language:

- **Useful, relevant**   The text provides the right information, making sure to explain the purpose of the UI element.
- **Easy to understand**   The text doesn't require thought or experimentation.
- **Explicit, specific**   The text doesn't undercommunicate.
- **Concise, efficient**   The text doesn't overcommunicate.
- **Good tone**   The text is friendly and has a good personality.

For an example of how incomprehensible abbreviations can be, the following example is from a major hotel's reservation system. Guess what the text at the top means.

FIGURE 3-25 Speak the user's language—without unnecessary abbreviations and acronyms.

If you must translate the text to explain it, it's not the user's language. How about using "Evolution Suite with 1 King Bed (nonsmoking)" instead?

Avoid using language that is ambiguous or misleading. For example, if you were asked to provide a password, what do you think you are being asked? The password for your account, right? Not necessarily…

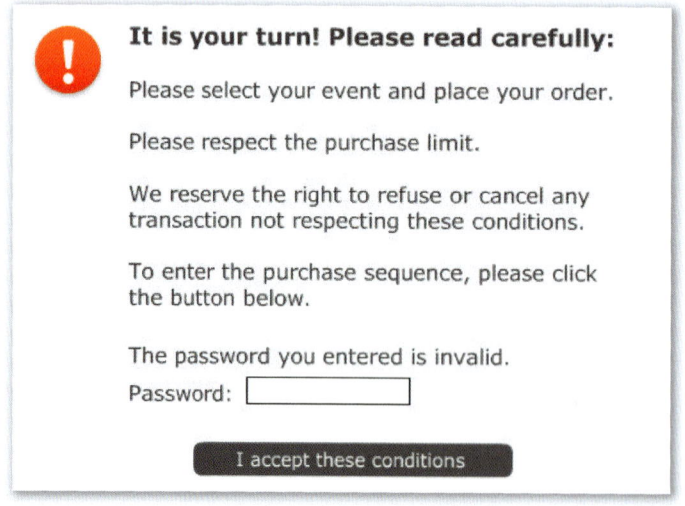

FIGURE 3-26 My password? I don't remember having an account. It turns out they are really asking for an Access Code to access a presale, making that the label to use.

Meeting expectations

Comprehensibility is the flip side of discoverability—users must understand the UI element to be confident that they are in the right place. **Even if the UI element's language is easily comprehensible, it might be confusing if it doesn't match their expectations.**

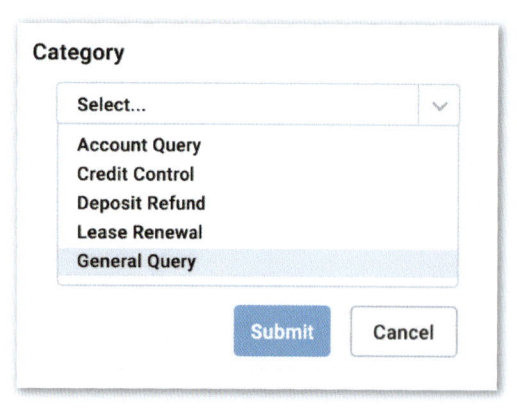

FIGURE 3-27 I need to file a work order because the heater in my apartment stopped working. Given these Category choices, I'm not thinking "General Query". Rather, I'm thinking "I must be in the wrong place because none of these options look right."

Chapter 3   The Eight Attributes of Intuitive UI

Appropriate use of icons

One possible solution to poor labeling is to not use language but to use icons instead. **A picture is worth a thousand words, right? Not if that picture is an icon. If it's an icon, it's worth one, two, or three words at most.** Disagree? See for yourself: what do these icons mean?

FIGURE 3-28 Try to come up with two or three words for each of these industry-specific icons. At least try to figure out the industry. Good luck!

There is an art to (and many, many guidelines for) designing effective icons, but ultimately icon design boils down to a single inconvenient truth, which I call *Everett's Rule for Custom Icons:*

> *Users understand the standard icons, but they won't understand your custom icons unless they are labeled.*

There is no science behind this rule, but I've found exceptions to be surprisingly rare. **If you design custom icons, you're going to have to label them to make them comprehensible.** While it might be a good idea to use custom icons to aid recognition, you will still need the text labels for comprehensibility.

FIGURE 3-29 Apparently, that wasn't the light switch!

Self-explanatory labels

There is a tradeoff between concise, single-word labels and self-explanatory, multiword labels. Traditionally, designers have favored conciseness (to work well on small, low-resolution screens), which is why there are so many single-word labels. **However, for modern, intuitive UIs, make the tradeoff in favor of being self-explanatory.**

Let's consider an example. The following buttons are from a reservation system. **What do you suppose these commands do in this View Reservation window?**

Comprehensibility – Appropriate use of icons   43

Because it's a modal window, users will assume that Cancel means *close the window*, but it really means *cancel this reservation*. I know this because I wanted to cancel the reservation and couldn't find the command anywhere.

Instead of clinging to single-word labels, let's add a word or two for clarity. Make the second button "Cancel Reservation" and all is well.

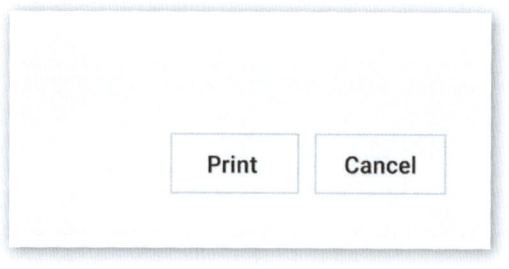

FIGURE 3-30 What do these commands do in a View Reservation window?

This example is so typical—often the difference between clarity and confusion is a single word. **If you would say that extra word in person to make things clear, put it in the UI label. Add the word!!**

Note that the purpose behind a command should influence labels far more than the technical details. Make sure it's clear why the user would want to use a command or choose an option, which might be different from the mechanical result. Here's an example:

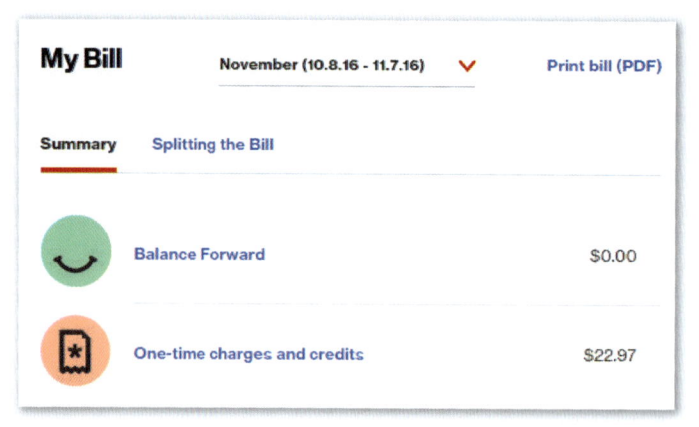

FIGURE 3-31 I'm looking all over for a detailed version of my cellphone bill but can't find it anywhere. Turns out, the Print Bill (PDF) command leads to that detailed version I'm looking for. Adding either "detailed" or "itemized" to the label would solve this problem. Add the word!

44   Chapter 3   The Eight Attributes of Intuitive UI

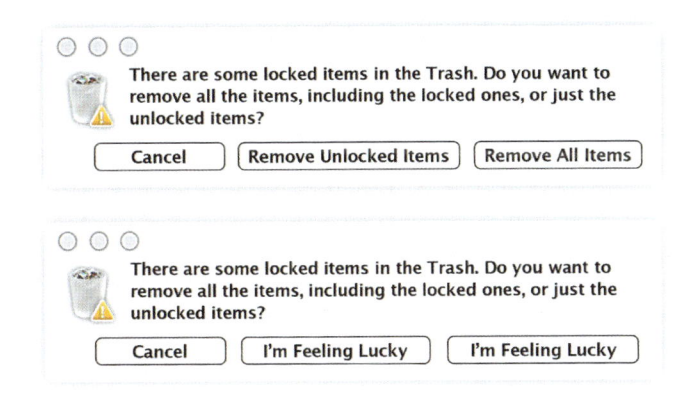

FIGURE 3-32 While these options are in plain language, the explanation is more mechanical than meaningful. Users are given no advice on which to choose or the consequences of their choices. My redesign on the bottom is equally uninformative.

Asking questions users know the answers to

When practical, provide all the information users need in context to make informed decisions. Prefer questions about what users likely already know (such as their names, email addresses, and phone numbers) instead of information that requires memorization (such as account numbers and access codes). Do you see the problem with the following Queen Mary tour options?

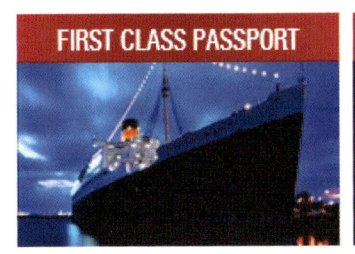

FIGURE 3-33 What is the difference between these tour options? The only difference given is the price, and even determining that requires some navigation and memorization.

Comprehensibility — Asking questions users know the answers to   45

As Don Norman says, prefer knowledge in the world over knowledge in the head. Gaining "knowledge in the head" requires memorization, experimentation, documentation, or training—and you now know what that means.

> **Best additional ways to evaluate comprehensibility**
>
> In addition to usability studies, consider performing an icon comprehension test, where you give participants your custom icons—unlabeled and out of context—and ask them to explain the purpose of each one. You'll be surprised how few custom icons people can explain accurately—this is likely true even for your own team. These tests are excellent proof that you need to label your custom icons!
>
> You can do a similar test to evaluate command and option labels by asking participants to explain the effect of each one and which they would choose. Again, prepare to be surprised.

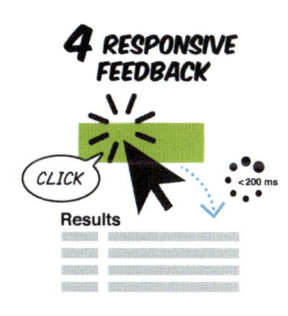

Responsive feedback

***Responsive feedback* is a clear, accurate, immediate indication of the current state of an interaction or the resulting state.** If an interaction has completed, users need a clear indication of completion and whether it succeeded or failed. Most feedback needs to be *responsive* to be useful—delayed feedback is inconvenient at best or misleading at worst.

Responsive feedback is a clear, accurate, immediate indication of the current state of an interaction or the resulting state.

Interaction feedback

For intuitive interaction, users need a clear, accurate, immediate indication of the interaction's current state to avoid confusion. For example, suppose the user taps a command button but there's no obvious feedback—what do you suppose the user will do? Tap again, right? Expect users to keep tapping away until they see some visible result. The reverse is also true: if users see feedback, they assume the interaction is taking place, so don't give such feedback unless that is actually the case.

To see how poor feedback leads to unintuitive interactions, consider a garage door remote control. When you press the button, the remote flashes an LED for feedback. However, that feedback indicates that a signal was sent by the transmitter, not that it was received by the door, so that feedback is largely useless—it really only indicates that the remote is working.

The feedback we use to determine that the signal was received is the movement of the door itself. But given that the garage-door-is-moving feedback is laggy rather than responsive, it's not uncommon to unnecessarily press the button again, which results in undoing the very thing we're trying to do! Now the door has been told to open and to

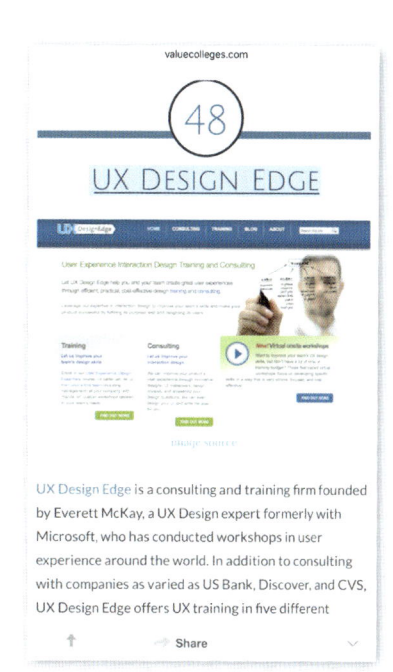

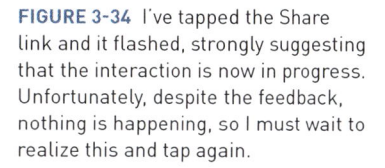

UX Design Edge is a consulting and training firm founded by Everett McKay, a UX Design expert formerly with Microsoft, who has conducted workshops in user experience around the world. In addition to consulting with companies as varied as US Bank, Discover, and CVS, UX Design Edge offers UX training in five different

FIGURE 3-34 I've tapped the Share link and it flashed, strongly suggesting that the interaction is now in progress. Unfortunately, despite the feedback, nothing is happening, so I must wait to realize this and tap again.

close, so the door stays closed. Having clear, accurate, immediate feedback (plus more forgiveness) would fix this problem.

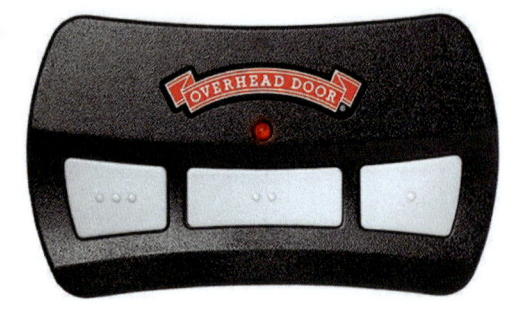

FIGURE 3-35 Garage door openers are often unintuitive because their feedback isn't responsive. Neither the tactile feedback of the button nor the flashing LED reliably mean that the door is opening.

Users need responsive feedback for both the current interaction and the resulting status. For interaction feedback, users need to know that the interaction has started and is either in progress or has completed. If successful results can be displayed quickly (under a second), the best feedback is to immediately (and clearly visibly) display the results. If more time is required (under 10 seconds), immediately display an activity indicator so that users know the task is in progress. If even more time is required (10+ seconds), display an accurate progress indicator with percentage complete feedback. Make sure that activity or progress indicators are displayed near the interaction.

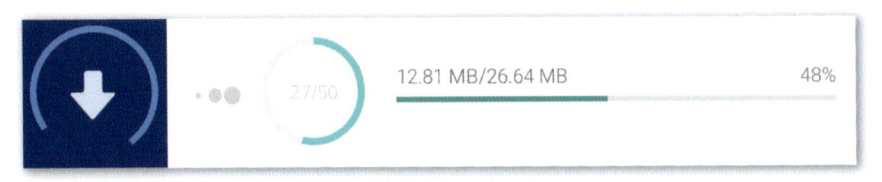

FIGURE 3-36 Examples of activity and progress indicators.

Status feedback

Indicating status—typically success, warning, failure; on vs. off; location—is an important part of responsive feedback. Status colors are often used in this feedback: green for success, yellow for warning, and red for failure. The interpretation of these colors is culturally dependent, but their meaning in the context of status is globally consistent due to the United Nations *Conventions on Road Signs and Signals*, so you don't have to localize them.

For accessibility, it's important to consider that not all users can distinguish every color. Approximately 8% of adult males have a form of *color confusion* (a more accurate term for color

48   Chapter 3   The Eight Attributes of Intuitive UI

blindness), so color must be used redundantly. **I recommend designing in monochrome and making sure that status indicators have a unique shape or text label for each state.** There are many tools that simulate the common forms of color confusion—an excellent way to make sure your designs are visually accessible.

Responsive feedback is important when changing status so that users know the status has in fact been changed.

FIGURE 3-37 Here I'm unmuting the microphone but the state change doesn't show until I move the mouse away from the mute button. See the problem?

While responsive feedback is usually visual, you can use sound or vibration (called *haptic*) as well. A challenge with sound is that it can be extremely intrusive (imagine a sound effect or Voice Command going off during a delicate social situation, like a wedding or live performance), whereas with haptic feedback the user must be holding or wearing the device to notice the feedback. **Because of these issues, sound and vibration are better as redundant forms of feedback and audio feedback should be optional and very easy to turn off.** For both, timely responsiveness is important. I can't tell you how many *new email* buzzes I've received on my iPhone to inform me of emails that I've already read.

Best additional ways to evaluate responsive feedback

During usability studies, consider periodically asking participants to explain the app's current state—without tapping or scrolling—especially if the status isn't contextual. A classic usability study evaluated a desktop app that featured a status bar (by the way, status bars aren't contextual) that stated, "There is $20 taped to the bottom of your chair. If you find it, it's yours!" Apparently, nobody found the money.

Predictability

5 PREDICTABILITY

Just what I expected

Predictability **determines whether target users can accurately predict the results of an interaction before they initiate it. An interaction is unpredictable if target users are surprised by the results or any of its side effects.** Discoverability, affordances, and comprehensibility set the stage before the interaction—predictability is the user's assessment of how well the interaction's results met expectations. Predictability is crucial for an intuitive interaction lifecycle because an interaction with surprising results or side effects is unlikely to achieve the user's goals.

> *Predictability determines whether target users can accurately predict the results of an interaction before they initiate it. An interaction is unpredictable if target users are surprised by its results or any of its side effects.*

An interaction can lead to unpredictable results in several ways. The results could be flat out wrong, users could be confused or misunderstand the design, or there could be a significant unexpected side effect even if the main outcome is as expected. Let's examine each type of unpredictability that contributes to a UI's unintuitiveness.

Unintuitive: Flat-out wrong

In this case, **an interaction is unpredictable because the behavior is just flat-out wrong—the outcome makes no sense for any likely scenario or prior experience.** For example, a Back command should return to the previously visited page (in its previous state), never clear or start over.

50   Chapter 3   The Eight Attributes of Intuitive UI

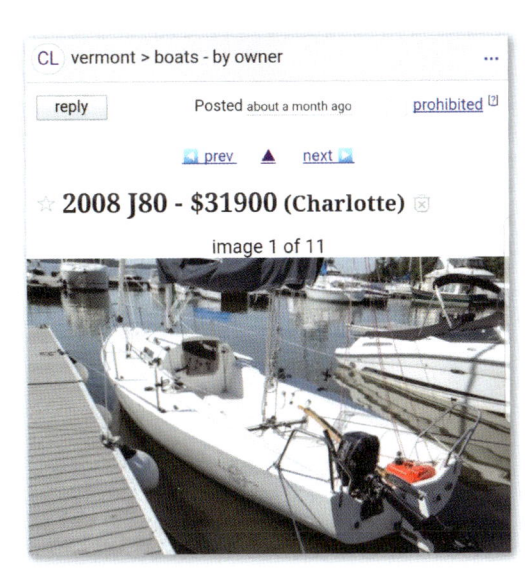

FIGURE 3-38 I'm browsing through a long list of search results, and I'm viewing an item. When I tap Back (which in Craigslist is actually the Up button), it returns me to the top of the search results. Wrong! Now I have to start over.

Unintuitive: Misunderstanding

In this case, **an interaction is unpredictable because users misunderstood it.** As mentioned, comprehensibility affects predictability, so possibly the label was poorly phrased or misleading, or perhaps the user didn't even read it.

When using a product, users have expectations—formally referred to as a *mental model*— for how they believe the product works. For example, some users associate air conditioning (AC) with cooling, so good luck getting them to choose AC to dehumidify a car in the middle of winter.

FIGURE 3-39 Many users believe AC means *make it cooler*, so they won't press an AC button in winter—no matter how fogged up the windows get.

Predictability — Unintuitive: Misunderstanding 51

For search, most experienced users expect that if a query has no matches, making the query more specific would be futile. (Technically, many consumer products perform "Boolean And" plus "begins with" searches.) Apparently not everyone got that memo.

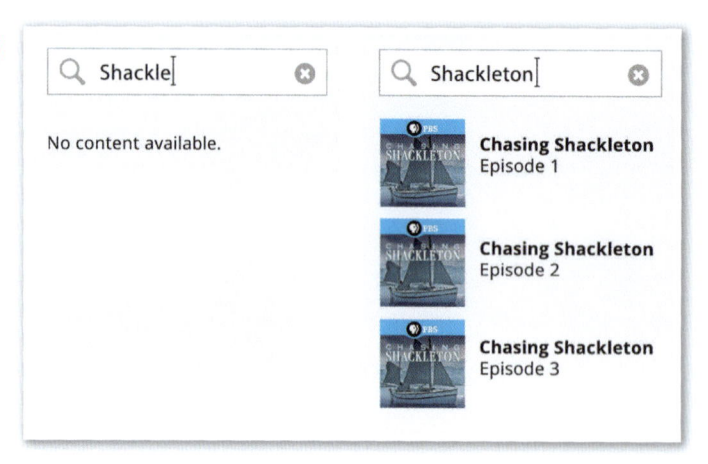

FIGURE 3-40 Searching for "shackle" has no matches, yet "shackleton" does. Surprise! Most users would have given up already.

Natural mapping helps avoid misunderstanding. *Natural mapping* **is when there is a clear relationship between what users want to do and how they should do it.** Moving physical objects without natural mapping can be extremely unintuitive. For example, a car seat controller should look like a car seat—as opposed to the old fashion unintuitive bank of switches.

FIGURE 3-41 Controlling a car seat with both natural and unnatural mapping.

There are two types of natural mapping: spatial and cultural. Spatial natural mapping is based on physics, so up is up and down is down, for example. By contrast, cultural natural mapping is based purely on cultural conventions, so left means back and right means forward based on Western reading order. Make sure you localize any cultural natural mapping in your app so that it is intuitive in other cultures.

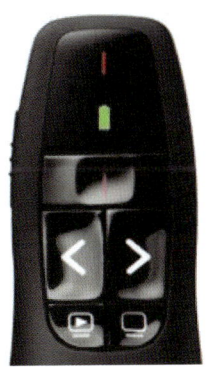

FIGURE 3-42 Which button on this presenter advances to the next slide? We read from left to right in Western cultures, so left is the past (back) and right is the future (next).

Make sure that any formats and units of measure are understood by your target users. Don't expect Americans to make decisions in terms of centimeters, for example. You might as well use cubits.

Unintuitive: Undesired side effects

In this case, **the overall result is predictable, but there are unexpected, frustrating, or even annoying side effects.** A *side effect* is a secondary, possibly unwanted, result of an interaction. For example, consider viewing your Inbox in portrait mode on a mobile device, rotating to landscape and then back again to portrait, and landing on a completely different part of your Inbox or even in an email. That would be unexpected!

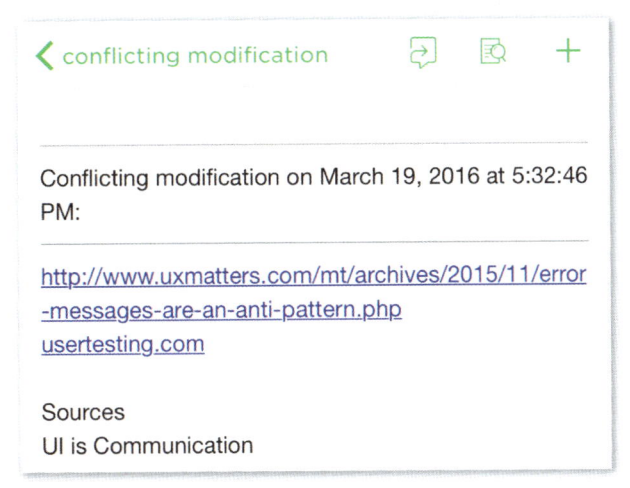

FIGURE 3-43 Evernote decided there is a conflicting modification to a note, so it invisibly tacks the new, correct document at the end, leaving me unaware of the problem.

Predictability – Unintuitive: Undesired side effects   53

By their very nature, side effects are often not a deliberate outcome of an interaction. Intuitive interactions need their side effects to at least make sense in the current context. **Users might not accurately predict an intuitive side effect, but they would definitely be confused by its absence.**

Tweet This!

Here are some common interaction side effects that are potentially unintuitive:

- **Moving**   Examples include navigating to different pages or scrolling the current page.

- **Resetting**   Examples include resetting searches, filters, sort orders, selections, input or view modes.

- **Deleting**   Examples include accepting a meeting invitation that results in deleting the invitation email as well.

- **Order**   When filling out a form, users expect their input to possibly affect fields below the current field but never above. Filling in a field should never clear previously filled out fields.

- **Changing modes**   Examples include changing the effect of taps or clicks. Make mode changes obvious, difficult to do accidentally, and very easy to revert.

Generally, when users start on a page with a certain state, navigate elsewhere to perform interactions that shouldn't change that state, and then return to the initial page, they expect the initial page's original state to be maintained. If that's not the case, make sure you have a solid justification based on satisfying users' goals.

> ### Best additional ways to evaluate predictability
>
> Usability studies are a great way to evaluate predictability. I recommend putting extra emphasis on situations where users correct, redo, or abandon tasks. Discovering that users frequently tap Cancel is a clear sign of poor predictability.
>
> There is a simple way to evaluate predictability during design reviews: ask participants to guess the outcome of an interaction before you show it or explain it. Many incorrect predictions are a clear sign of a problem. Try this technique—it's amazingly effective! You will be surprised by how many design problems you find.

Chapter 3   The Eight Attributes of Intuitive UI

Efficiency

***Efficiency*, in our context, determines whether the design helps target users perform their top tasks without unnecessary interaction or repetition.** If a design interferes with user goals by requiring difficult, unnecessary, or highly repetitive interaction or by poor error handling, users will describe it as unintuitive (along with clunky and cumbersome) and rightly so. Generally, efficiency is broad enough for a book of its own (and that's on my to-do list!), so here I'll focus only on those areas where efficiency directly affects intuitiveness.

Efficiency determines whether the design helps target users perform their top tasks without unnecessary interaction or repetition.

Unintuitive: Inefficient interaction

Tasks with inefficient interaction are often the result of poor control sizing and poor layout. The interactive part of a UI element should be at least as large as its container/affordance.

FIGURE 3-44 Make the entire button interactive, not just the label. The example on the left is incorrect.

For small targets, consider making the interactive target larger—possibly much larger—than the visible UI element.

FIGURE 3-45 If I tap anywhere near the close command in the upper left corner of a tab, my intent is clear—I want to close that tab. But the touch target is so small, I constantly select the tab instead. For smaller UI elements, consider making interactive targets larger than their visible area.

For links, normally only the link text itself is interactive, so choose large link labels for easy-to-acquire targets. "Go" is a poor link choice, for example. If a link is used instead of a command button, consider sizing the interactive target to be the size of a button instead of just the label.

FIGURE 3-46 The iOS Clock app uses a link instead of a button for the Stop command, and it's too small to be a comfortable touch target. To make it easier to turn off an alarm (especially under duress), use a large button instead.

Chapter 3 The Eight Attributes of Intuitive UI

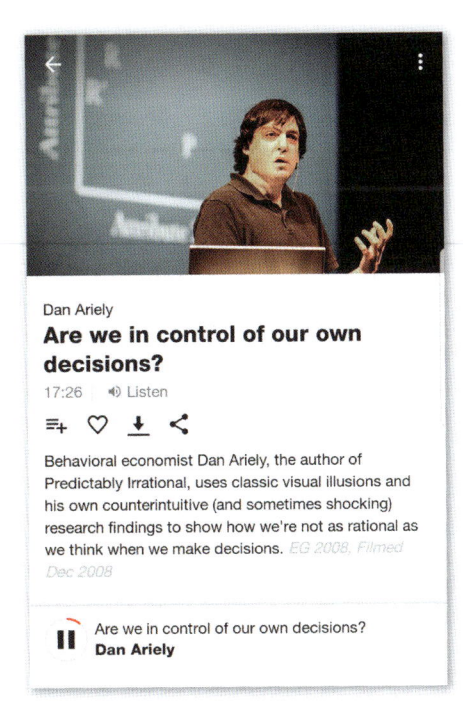

FIGURE 3-47 Sticky menu bars and controllers are a great way to maintain context. Here, the TED app provides a sticky media controller so that you can explore while a video is playing.

Also, make sure that UI elements that are frequently used together are placed together. Users shouldn't have to move across the screen or scroll to perform routine interaction combinations.

Unintuitive: Unnecessary interaction

Routine tasks should require commensurate interaction. For example, while I appreciate date pickers for choosing recent or upcoming dates that I'm not too sure of (like departure and arrival dates), they only get in the way for choosing known dates (like my birthday) because going back that many years can be a chore. Users should just be able to type in known, far away dates.

FIGURE 3-48 If users (older users especially) don't discover the secret passageway for selected dates (tapping the header), they are going to spend some quality time tapping the previous month arrow button. (Doing the math: 50 x 12 = 600 taps for a 50-year-old.) I know my birthday without a calendar, so let me just type it in.

Appropriate defaults

You don't always exactly know what your users want. (If you do, you should just do it!) **If you know with reasonable probability (based on the current context) what your users want, provide that value or result as a default.** **Doing so not only makes the interaction more efficient but also less error-prone.** That said, make sure any defaults are valid. Accepting a default should never result in error, loss, or harm (or worse—see the sidebar at the end of the chapter). Even though you might not know what users want the first time they perform a task, you should have a better idea any subsequent time because the next input is very often based on or related to the previous input.

FIGURE 3-49 Consider first-time use a special exception for having appropriate defaults. Your app will know more on subsequent use. Here, after 12 years and many searches, Yelp still assumes that I'm in San Francisco, which is annoying. Even without location awareness, my last location is a better default.

58   Chapter 3   The Eight Attributes of Intuitive UI

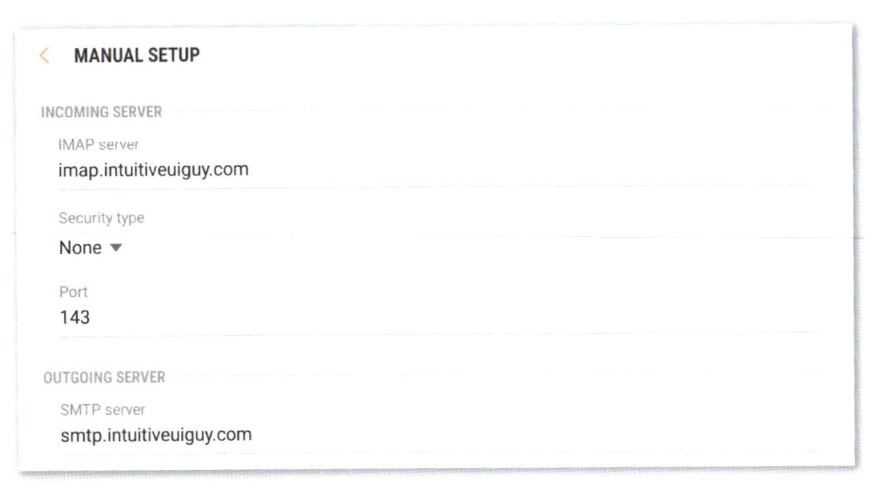

> **MANUAL SETUP**
>
> INCOMING SERVER
> IMAP server
> imap.intuitiveuiguy.com
>
> Security type
> None ▼
>
> Port
> 143
>
> OUTGOING SERVER
> SMTP server
> smtp.intuitiveuiguy.com

FIGURE 3-50 I'm setting up a new email account. My settings? Aside from the address and password, exactly the same as all my other accounts. Yet, I must memorize or write down the details and set up everything manually. Appropriate defaults based on prior input would make this task easy.

FIGURE 3-51 For a good example, I love how Roku temporarily displays subtitles for an Instant Replay. The top scenario for the rewind: misunderstanding what was just said.

If using your app feels like the movie *Groundhog Day*, it needs better defaults.

That said, knowing what your users want with *reasonable probability* needs some specificity. If you know what the user input will be with, say, 90% confidence, that of course would be an excellent default. Given that it is often easier to change a default than to type in a value from scratch, that probability bar can be much, much lower, especially for long and complex input such as a mailing address. The tradeoff is the potential for saving effort vs. the user having to clear input or even the potential embarrassment or annoyance of incorrect defaults. Even a default with only 20% confidence would be appropriate if the potential for saving effort were large and any downside small.

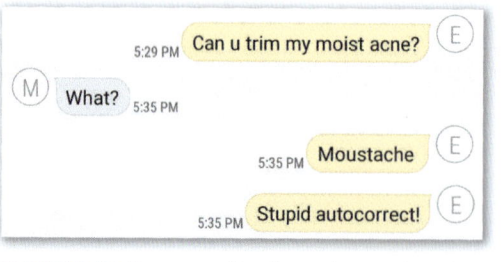

FIGURE 3-52 The more effort for an interaction, the lower the bar for appropriate defaults. But consider the potential risk, embarrassment, and/or annoyance if you get it wrong.

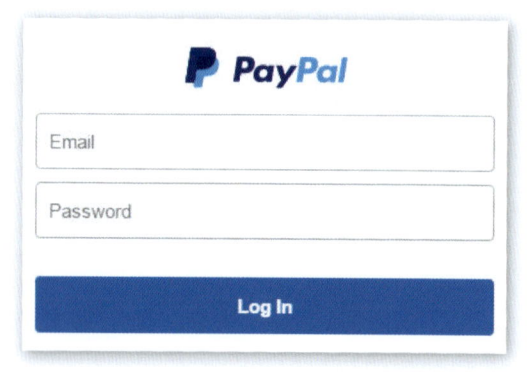

FIGURE 3-53 Passwords aren't a good place for defaults.

Some notable exceptions: don't default private information like passwords, social security numbers, or credit card numbers, and don't use defaults to bias input that should be unbiased. Also, don't draw drastic conclusions based on the current context.

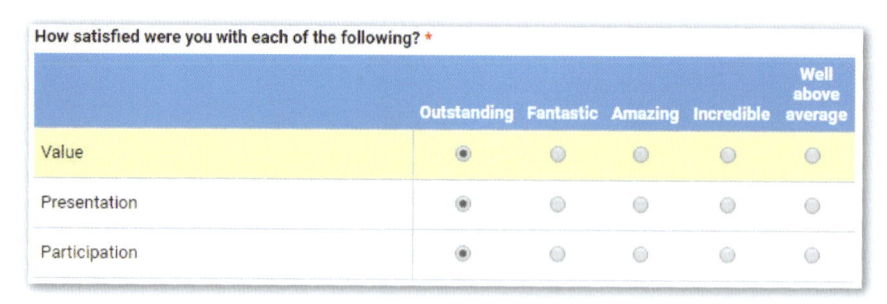

FIGURE 3-54 Customer surveys should be unbiased—defaults can result in bias.

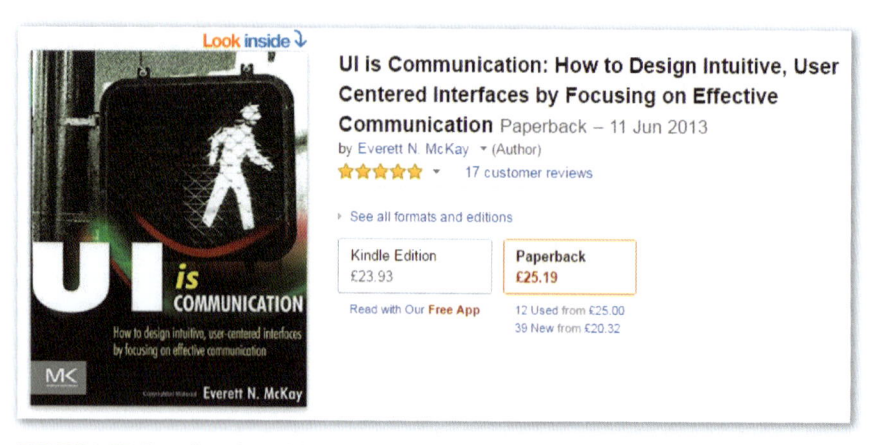

FIGURE 3-55 Traveling abroad isn't quite the same as moving abroad. Even though I'm in the UK now, I would prefer to pay in U.S. dollars, please. Don't read too much into an IP address.

60   Chapter 3   The Eight Attributes of Intuitive UI

Unintuitive: Forgetting or not using user input

There's often an even better default than the ones I just mentioned: the input the user entered mere moments ago. Unintuitive UIs ask users questions but then fail to take full advantage of the answers. **If user input is important enough to ask for, it's important enough to remember and reuse.** For example, it's common to require personal information during registration, such as name, email, phone number, address, etc., and then later require users to manually provide the same information elsewhere (for, say, how to be notified). At the very least, previously entered info should be used as the default.

But it gets worse. It's not uncommon for user input to get cleared due to some problem or the input not being entered in exactly the right sequence. And the more complex the input, the more likely this will happen, resulting in what I call *Everett's Law of Complex Input*:

The more complex the input, the more likely users will have to enter it more than once.

FIGURE 3-56 Guess how many times I had to enter my 16 character Lufthansa user ID to access my account. Try four. (Two PIN tries, password reset, new password.) Doing the math, that's 64 characters' worth of input just for the first step. Don't be in a hurry to clear user input—it's rude!

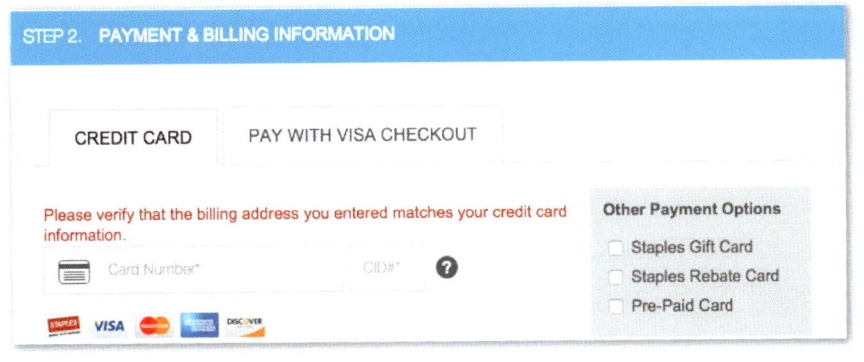

FIGURE 3-57 Wait...so there's a problem with my billing address...and you clear my valid card number? Rude!

Error handling

Poor error handling is another topic broad enough for a book of its own (also on my list!), so instead **let's focus on three error-handling topics that have the most impact on intuitive UIs: uninformative error messages, missing error handling, and unnecessary messages.**

It's hardly news to point out that many error messages are poorly written. Effective error messages state a clear problem, a meaningful explanation of the cause, and a likely and practical solution. (Please note that *Contact your internet service provider* is probably not a practical solution.) An intuitive error message is specific so that users don't have to think or experiment to figure out the specific problem.

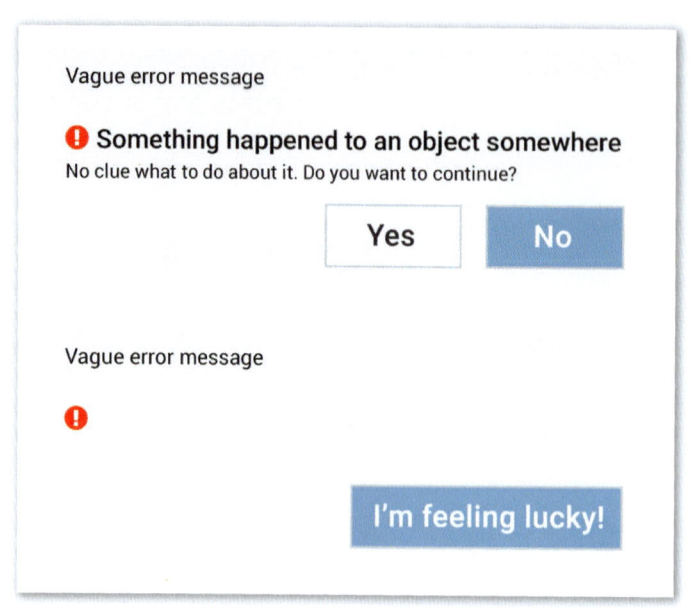

Unintuitive

Vague error message

❗ **Something happened to an object somewhere**
No clue what to do about it. Do you want to continue?

Yes   No

Vague error message

❗

I'm feeling lucky!

FIGURE 3-58 For most users, these two error messages are identical.

Some designers believe that error messages are *the* worst user experience and the best error message is no error message. But this is wrong—having confused users or making significant mistakes is far worse. We certainly want to avoid unnecessary messages, but intuitive UIs need *necessary* error messages. Otherwise, users are forced to think and experiment to deduce the problem on their own.

What's a necessary error message? Here's a simple test: Write the error message (as best you can). If it's informative, consider it necessary; if not, eliminate it. I will discuss necessary vs. unnecessary error messages a bit more in Chapter 4.

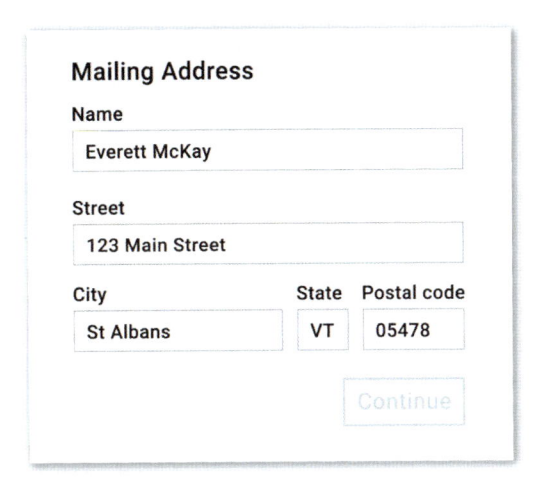

FIGURE 3-59 That's my mailing address (more or less), yet the Continue button is disabled for some reason. The address looks good to me—time for some experimentation? Please, just tell me what the problem is with a helpful message!

But it's true—there are many unnecessary error messages out there. If a condition is really just routine status, present it as status (contextually) rather than force users to dismiss a modal error window. If you must use an error window, be sure to display it only once—there's nothing more annoying than dismissing the same error message repeatedly.

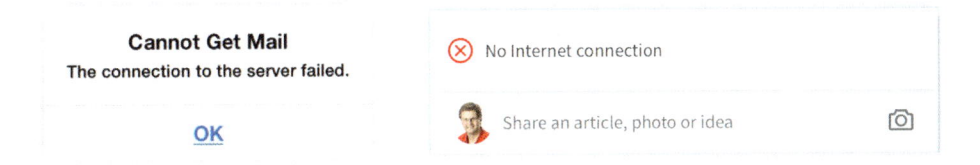

FIGURE 3-60 Thanks for telling me...eight times in a row. Unnecessary errors like the one on the left can be really annoying. Display status contextually, as on the right, rather than displaying it as an error that requires dismissing.

Appropriate constraints

Constraints can be used to limit input to valid values. Generally, constrained input controls (like lists and sliders) are preferable to unconstrained input controls (like text boxes). If a choice is impossible in the current state, it is more efficient and less error-prone if users can't select it. But be careful—if it's 12:01 a.m., it is still possible to reserve a hotel room for the previous night, as anyone stuck at an airport can attest.

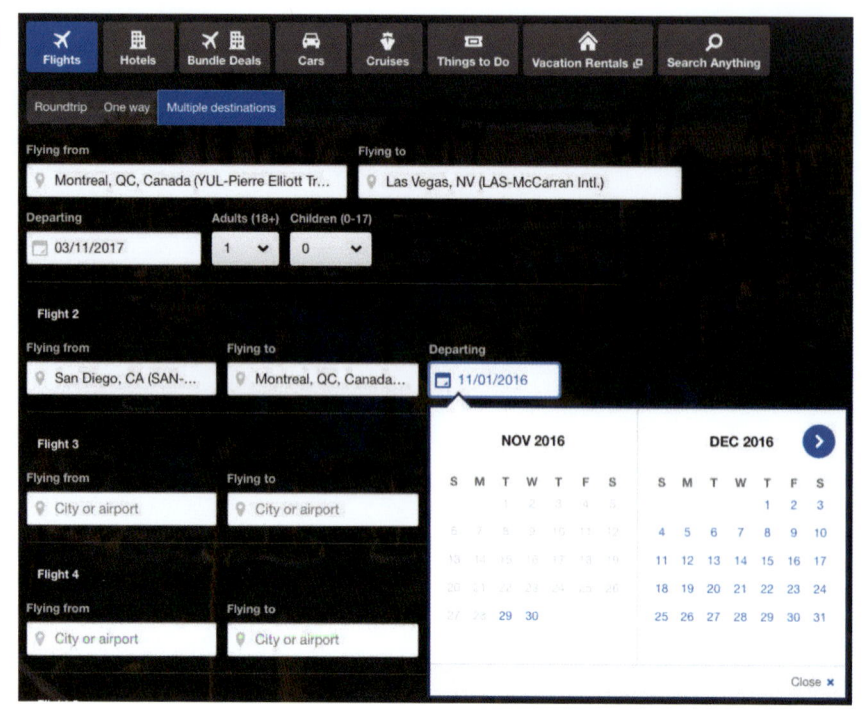

FIGURE 3-61 It's impossible to return from a flight before you leave, but you would never know that from some reservation apps. A more intuitive design would constrain the return date to the departure date and after.

Unintuitive: Technical failure

Sometimes interaction results are constrained unnecessarily. That is, users enter input that is essentially correct—their intent is clear and the input is unambiguous—yet the interaction fails due to some technical detail. In this scenario, the interaction fails only in the technical sense.

The most common example is when apps fuss over minor formatting, such as separators. Complex input (like phone, credit card, and ID numbers) is often required to have an exact separator format and is rejected even if the user enters a valid value.

FIGURE 3-62 I'm trying to paste a valid phone number, but Skype supplies the country code and insists on having input without one—which I can't fix in the app itself!

64   Chapter 3   The Eight Attributes of Intuitive UI

Another common example is when apps fuss over capitalization/case, punctuation, and whitespace, such as unnecessary leading or trailing spaces. It serves no purpose to have case-sensitive CAPTCHAs and coupon codes.

FIGURE 3-63 OK, technically these email addresses aren't the same, but email addresses aren't case-sensitive. Furthermore, the keyboard defaulted to uppercase for that first character, so I didn't even type them differently.

FIGURE 3-64 I typed the coupon code correctly—except that it was supposed to be all uppercase. Why does case matter for a coupon code? And good to know that it's error code 620 and not 621 or 619. Oh, and thanks for clearing my input on error.

One last example is when search is overly fussy, returning results only for literal exact matches. This problem includes searches that can't handle different spellings (like Wi-Fi vs. WiFi), similar words (like car vs. auto), plurals vs. singular, common abbreviations (like USA vs. United States), or common misspellings. **We need to change the old saying: almost only counts in horseshoes, hand grenades, and intuitive search.**

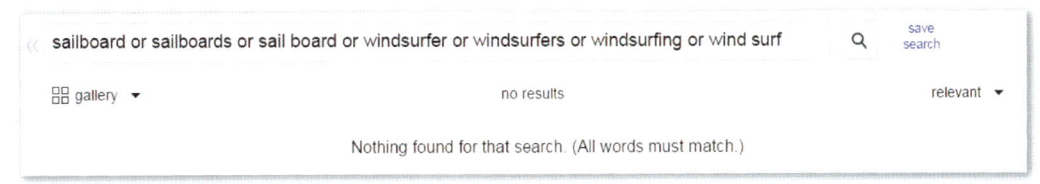

FIGURE 3-65 To find sailboard equipment on craigslist, you must search for sailboard, sailboards, sail board, windsurfer, windsurfers, windsurfing, wind surf. But one at a time because it doesn't support Boolean searches.

Intuitive searches return the closest matches rather than no results.

Efficiency — Unintuitive: Technical failure   65

Intuitive

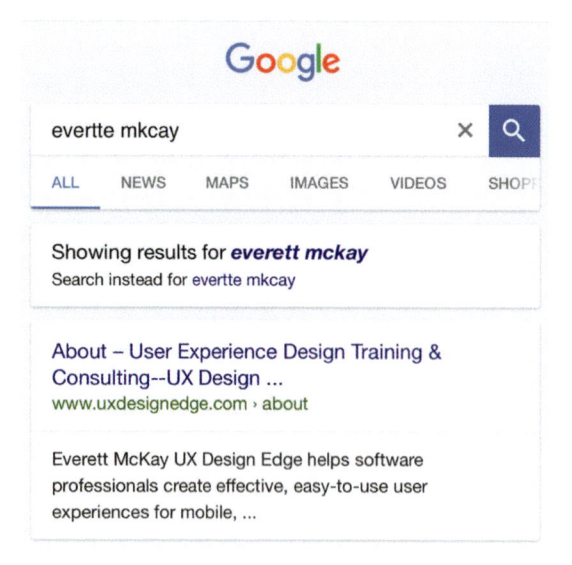

FIGURE 3-66 Google always returns the closest matches, even if you misspell the query.

Unintuitive: Unnecessary restrictions/annoyances

Unnecessary restrictions are those that interfere with users achieving their goals by requiring unnecessary interaction or repetition. A good example is requiring users to select a single item at a time when the task requires selecting multiple items.

Unintuitive

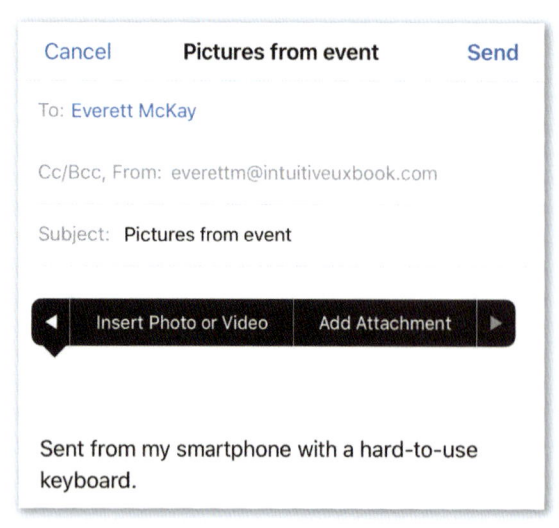

FIGURE 3-67 I want to attach several photos to this email, but I can select only one at a time.

66   Chapter 3   The Eight Attributes of Intuitive UI

An all-too-common annoyance is to fill out a page in order, only to have a later setting clear your previous entries.

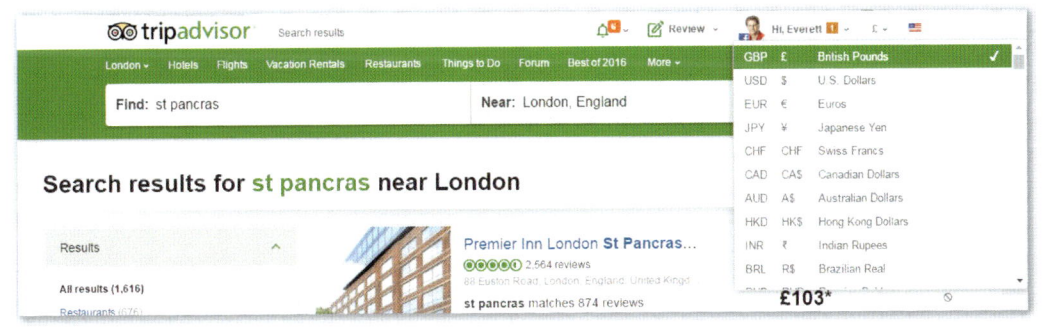

FIGURE 3-68 I set the hotel and location and then change the currency...which resets the hotel and location.

Another unnecessary annoyance is to have to dismiss a pile of messages when only one message is really necessary.

FIGURE 3-69 The first of many reminders for tomorrow. A single consolidated reminder would be sufficient.

Unintuitive: Contextual stupidity

When possible, consider the user's context and do the right thing for that context.

FIGURE 3-70 This message wouldn't be so bad—if I hadn't initiated Airplane Mode mere moments ago.

Efficiency — Unintuitive: Contextual stupidity   **67**

> **Best additional ways to evaluate efficiency**
>
> Usability testing is a great way to evaluate efficiency. During usability studies, look out for unnecessarily repeated interactions, unnecessary typing, poor default values, users having to constantly fix incorrect default behaviors, and confusion or annoyance caused by poor error handling.

7 FORGIVENESS

Forgiveness

***Forgiveness* assesses whether an interaction prevents mistakes, minimizes the negative impact of mistakes, or makes mistakes easy to recover from.** Intuitive apps assume that small mistakes are common, and they accommodate these mistakes. By contrast, unintuitive apps are not forgiving and result in a significant loss of work or inconvenience, such as forcing the user to completely redo the task. Unforgiving apps tend to result in many mistakes incorrectly attributed to "human error."

> *Forgiveness assesses whether an interaction prevents mistakes, minimizes the negative impact of mistakes, or makes mistakes easy to recover from.*

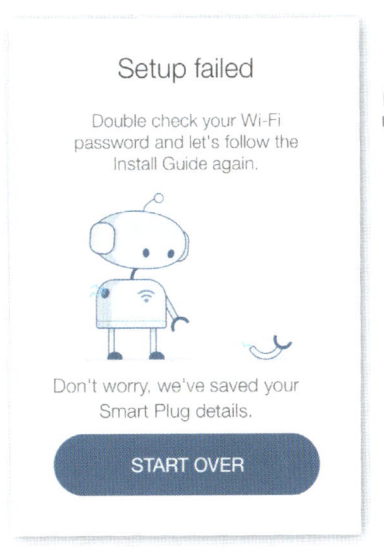

FIGURE 3-71 Start Over—the official onramp to the unhappy path.

Often teams evaluate their designs by assuming users know and stay on the *happy path*—where users understand and perform tasks perfectly—which is unrealistic for all but the most trivial tasks. I call this design approach *happy path myopia*. Because users make small mistakes all the time, they are as likely to be off the happy path as on it. To make a UI intuitive, the unhappy path needs to be designed just as carefully as the happy one, but in practice it is rarely considered. You should consider lack of forgiveness in your app a design flaw—it's your mistake as a designer, not the user's.

Preventing mistakes

The best approach to forgiveness is to prevent mistakes in the first place. It's impossible to prevent all mistakes generally, but we can and should prevent users from *easily* making mistakes. Perhaps the best example is that most buttons take effect on tap-release or mouse-button-up instead of tap-down or mouse-button-down. Doing so gives users an opportunity to abandon an unwanted command by moving off the control before release.

Forgiveness – Preventing mistakes **69**

FIGURE 3-72 Try a long press on the Clear command in a Calculator app. Note that the clear doesn't happen until your release.

Where do you suppose is the worst possible place for an unconfirmed Trash command on the iPhone?

FIGURE 3-73 The worst place for a Trash command? How about directly over the Home button, where it is begging to be tapped accidentally when you mean to press the Home button. If you are an iPhone user, you have probably done this many times without even realizing it.

For touch-based interaction, targets need to be at least 9mm square for accuracy and even larger for comfortable, mistake-preventing interaction. Prefer big, fingertip-sized targets whenever practical. Consult your platform's guidelines for additional sizing recommendations.

70   Chapter 3   The Eight Attributes of Intuitive UI

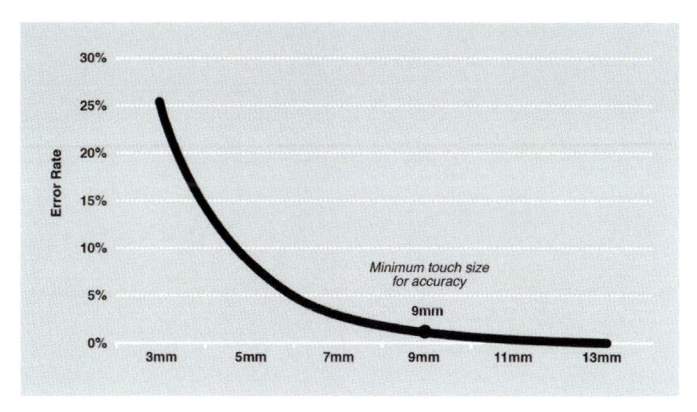

FIGURE 3-74 For accurate touch-based interactions, 9mm square is considered the minimum size. Larger is better.

For touch-based interaction, spacing can be as important as sizing. **Put enough space between interactive UI elements to prevent accidental touch.** Again, consult your platform's guidelines for spacing recommendations.

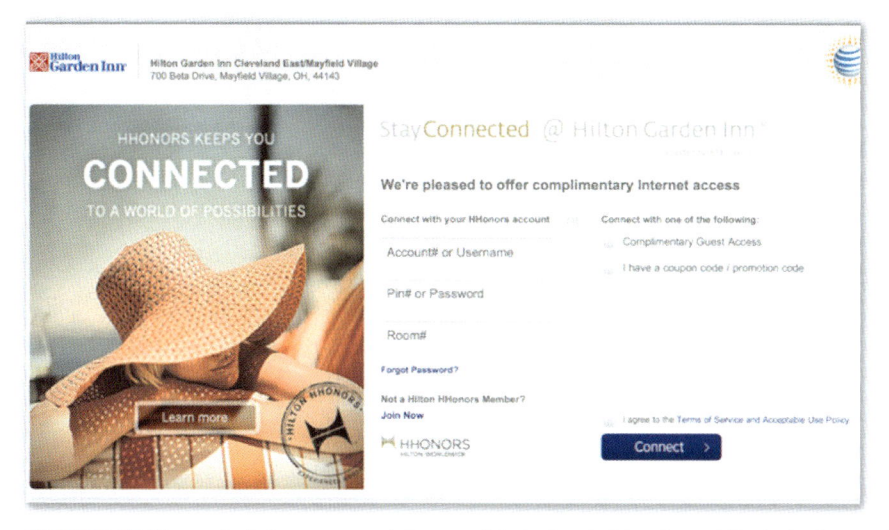

FIGURE 3-75 The controls here are much too small to be touch-friendly, and the lack of space between the Terms checkbox and the Connect button make this screen hazard-prone.

Often, having a margin for error is literal, not just figurative—you need to provide a physical margin when the user being off by a few pixels makes an interaction hazard-prone.

Forgiveness – Preventing mistakes   71

FIGURE 3-76 Suppose you are trying to resize this photo by dragging the grabber in the lower right, but you are off by a couple pixels. You end up moving the image instead. Make touch targets at least 9x9mm, regardless of their visible size.

Another important way to prevent mistakes is to confirm destructive actions and put them out of easy reach.

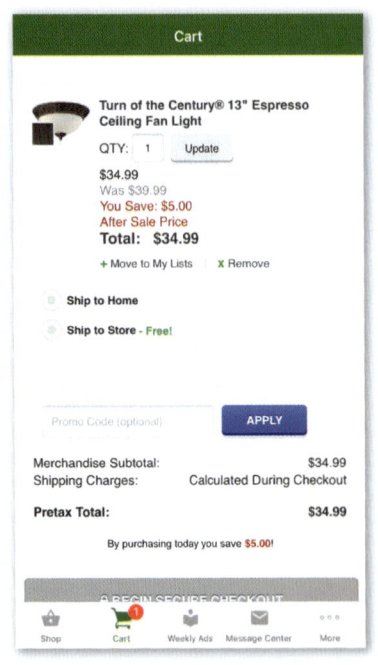

FIGURE 3-77 The Remove (from shopping cart) command (which isn't confirmed) is placed right where users are likely to swipe to scroll the shopping cart.

72   Chapter 3   The Eight Attributes of Intuitive UI

FIGURE 3-78 The most destructive command on a calculator is AC (All Clear), which for the iPhone requires two taps instead of one (the first tap is Clear, as shown on the left). This ensures that the command is deliberate and eliminates the need for a dedicated button at the same time.

FIGURE 3-79 I love accessing my phone using Bluetooth in my car, but answering a call doesn't always have responsive feedback so I occasionally press Answer twice. The screen reveals what the second button press does instead of answer. Put destructive actions out of easy reach!

Undo

Undo is the classic forgiveness feature, and your app should provide Undo whenever practical. Unfortunately, it's not always practical to provide Undo—often for performance reasons—as we'll explore in detail in Chapter 5, so your app needs to be forgiving in other ways.

Another challenge with Undo is that its implementation is often unintuitive because its results are not predictable. Moderately experienced users should be able to accurately predict

Forgiveness – Undo 73

the effect of an Undo command. And if your app does anything automatically, make sure any immediately applied Undo command undoes the automatic effect.

Use a broad interpretation of Undo. Don't just think about an Undo command—also make sure that every uncommitted command has an opposite. Every OK needs a Cancel, every Add needs a Remove, every Forward needs a Back, every Accept needs a No Thanks, every Open needs a Close, and so on.

Easy recovery

Once a user makes a mistake, make it easy to fix. Make items easy to edit, make it easy to enter edit mode, easy to abandon changes if unwanted, and easy to go back where the user came from, without completely starting over. History features are very forgiving. **Be sure to not clear erroneous input—let users choose to clear instead. For multistep tasks, always have a Back.**

FIGURE 3-80 Here, I'm not getting the search results I want, but it's easy to change my inputted text, clear my input and start over, or cancel my interaction altogether.

74   Chapter 3   The Eight Attributes of Intuitive UI

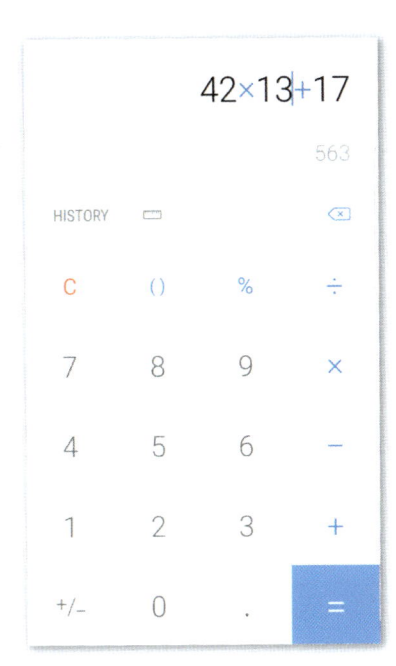

FIGURE 3-81 Oops, I made a mistake in entering the calculation, which I can easily edit without starting over.

> ### Best additional ways to evaluate forgiveness
>
> Usability studies are a great way to evaluate forgiveness. I recommend putting extra emphasis on situations where users make small mistakes and examining the effort required for them to recover. If your app supports Undo, be sure to test for predictability. To get users off the happy path in your usability studies, consider giving instructions that are slightly confusing or tasks where mistakes are likely. If users must completely start over because of a small mistake, consider that a failure.
>
> Another great way to get users off the happy path is with Streamlined Cognitive Walkthroughs, which I describe in Chapter 7.

Explorability

8 EXPLORABILITY

Explorability determines whether target users can use your app without fear of getting lost or making significant mistakes. A good antonym for explorable is *hazard-prone*. (By contrast, a good antonym for forgiveness is *error-prone*.) **An explorable app builds the user's confidence and sense of mastery. Explorability is a higher-level attribute than the others—it's possible for an app to have the other seven attributes yet still feel unintuitive if it lacks explorability.** Top causes for poor explorability are confusing, nonstandard navigation models and unclear, nonstandard commit models.

> *Explorability determines whether target users can use your app without fear of getting lost or accidentally making mistakes.*

An app is hazard-prone when users are literally reluctant to touch it. You watch them try to do a task and their hands recoil and they say, "Whoa! Wait a minute! What just happened?" Explorability is potentially a very large topic space, so let's frame it by considering two of the original Apple Macintosh human interface design principles: direct manipulation and user in control.

Confirm destructive actions

We already covered the need to confirm destructive actions in the "Forgiveness" section, but the examples there were fairly routine (such as accidentally clearing a calculation). For actions with significant consequences, explorability requires both confirmation and awareness. **It should be impossible for a user to permanently delete a photo album, for example, without a confirmation that demands the user's attention.** (This is an unfortunate accident that I have personally experienced. It was surprisingly easy to do.)

The challenge is that over-confirming leads to habituation. **Verifying everything is practically the same as inconveniently verifying nothing—users quickly learn to ignore routine confirmations. The best solution:** Draw special attention to actions with significant consequences, and don't bother confirming insignificant actions. Make the safest choice the default.

Tweet This!

I recommend such confirmations even if there is an Undo (such as a Trash Can or Recycle Bin to recover the files). The reason: Undo is helpful only if the user is aware that there is something to undo. Significant irreversible destructive actions should require users to make two consecutive mistakes, not just one.

FIGURE 3-82 Which confirmation will get the user's attention?

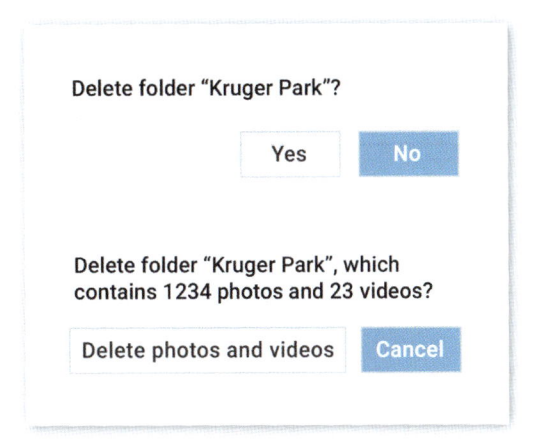

FIGURE 3-83 If the "New folder" folder is empty, don't even bother asking!

Direct manipulation vs. accidental manipulation

Direct manipulation **is when users interact directly with an object's representation on the screen, as opposed to indirectly through some UI proxy (like a menu, dialog box, or command line).** Direct manipulation originally referred to mouse-based interaction, and it is even more direct now with touch-based interaction—the user is in direct physical contact with an on-screen object.

But where there is direct manipulation, there is the potential for *accidental manipulation*. It's important for interactions—especially touch-based interactions—to be deliberate rather than accidental. Having interactive UI elements without clear affordances or having tap targets that are excessively large invites accidental manipulation. This, of course, is why smartphones are activated by a deliberate gesture such as swipe.

My advice is to be very careful with using gestures, especially edge swipes, double taps, and long presses—these are the most likely gestures to be done accidentally.
When using these gestures, consider the likelihood of them being performed accidentally and what users will need to do to recognize the situation and correct it. Supporting more gestures is not necessarily better!

FIGURE 3-84 Unlocking a phone is a deliberate interaction—it's hard to swipe a small target with your butt!

Explorability — Direct manipulation vs. accidental manipulation

User in control

User in control simply means that the user, not your app, is ultimately in control. This principle suggests that we need to be very careful with automatic behaviors and side effects. Still, for convenience and efficiency, we don't want users to have to do everything manually, especially when we are almost certain what they want to do. **Google's Android guidelines offer the perfect compromise:**

Decide for me, but let me have the final say.

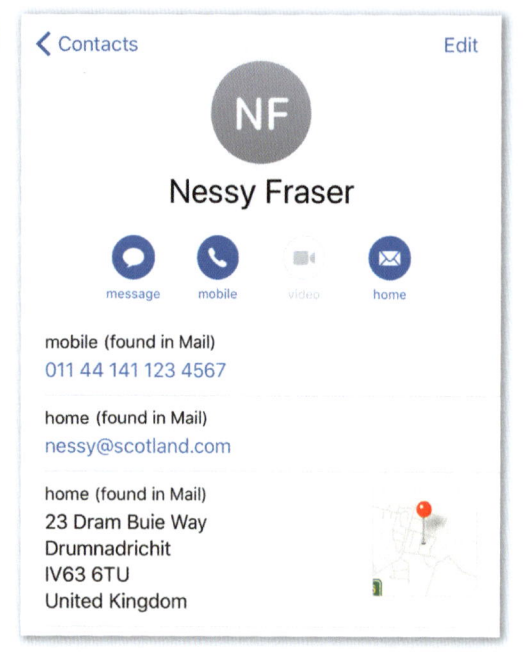

FIGURE 3-85 My iPhone found this contact information in an email—I didn't set it up myself. Consequently, I have to choose explicitly to use this phone number, giving me the final say on an otherwise completely automatic action.

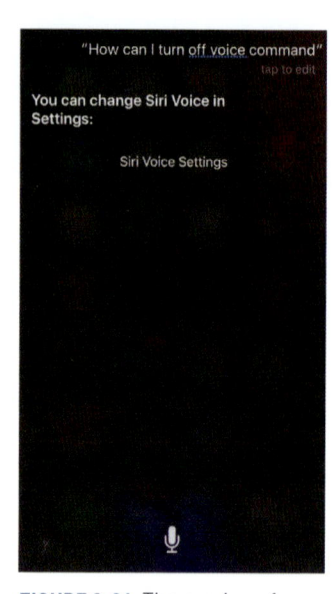

FIGURE 3-86 The number of times I have invoked the Voice Command screen: hundreds. The number of times I have done so intentionally: zero! Long press on the home button is way too easy to do accidentally.

Clear navigation models

For explorability, users need to be able to navigate your UI without fear of getting lost or getting stuck. Web browsers set the standard for modern navigation. While you don't necessarily need to use web-style navigation, **you need to make sure your app has these navigation essentials:**

- A clear, visually obvious way to get to the next step or complete a task (and unless the task is using a hub and spoke navigation, Back is not an obvious way to get to the next step).

- A clear, visually obvious way to return to the previous step.

- An obvious way to abandon a task.

- An obvious way to return home (where *home* is a known starting point).

For touch-based interaction, consider gestures that support these essentials to be shortcuts—there needs to be visible controls for these types of navigation on the screen as well.
If your app is missing any of these essentials, users won't be able to navigate with confidence.

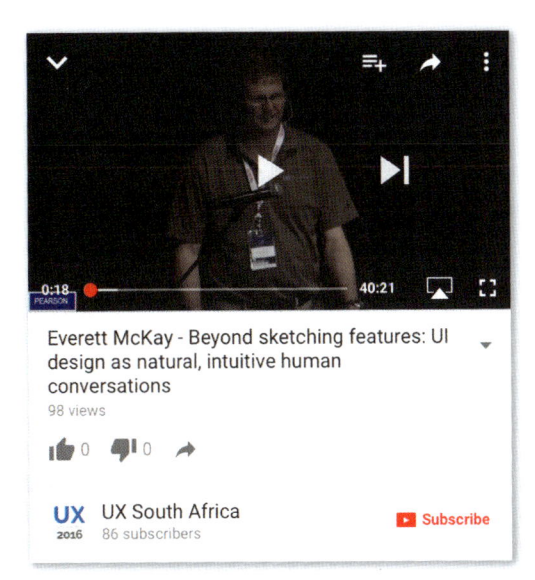

FIGURE 3-87 How do I get back to the previous page? I'm not sure. There's no Back button, just some kind of Down button.

Clear commit models

An app's *commit model* determines how changes are committed or discarded and how users navigate to the next step in a task. There are two common models: *explicit save* and *instant commit*. Explicit save means that users must explicitly save any changes or they will be abandoned, whereas instant commit means any changes are applied immediately.

Although either model can support Undo, the explicit save model is the better choice when users need to be able to explore without fear. Your photo editor app better use explicit save or I'm not using it!

For your app to be explorable, you need to choose the right commit model and make it visually obvious which model you are using—at a glance, without scrolling. Support Undo and Revert as necessary. Users should never be surprised to discover which commit model is being used. The worst possible surprise: a complex multi-step explicit-commit-at-every-step task with the commit buttons below the fold, where the user completes the task only to discover that nothing was saved. (Many of us who have configured a wireless router can attest to this pain.)

Intuitive

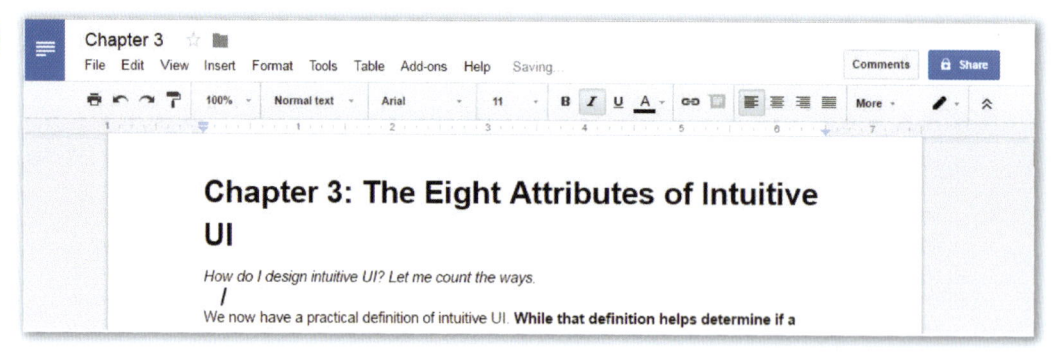

FIGURE 3-88 Google Docs uses instant commit and makes it obvious from the status on the menu bar. It's a bit subtle, but notice that it says "Saving..." at the right of the menus.

Building confidence

Tweet This!

Confidence *is a feeling users have when they believe that they are doing the right thing and their goals are being satisfied.* **Users need to feel confident when using your app—especially for tasks that have consequences.**

Unintuitive

Let's consider a simple example: You need to wake up at 4 a.m. tomorrow morning (Thursday) for an early flight. Did you set your alarm correctly? How many ways could you do it wrong?

There are several mistakes here. It's set for 4 p.m. on the wrong day. Worse, the battery is just about gone, so the settings won't matter. How about now in Figure 3-90?

Notice how the redundancy serves to make sure that users are doing what they want and consequently builds their confidence.

FIGURE 3-89 Is this intuitive? Should you be confident in this alarm?

80   Chapter 3   The Eight Attributes of Intuitive UI

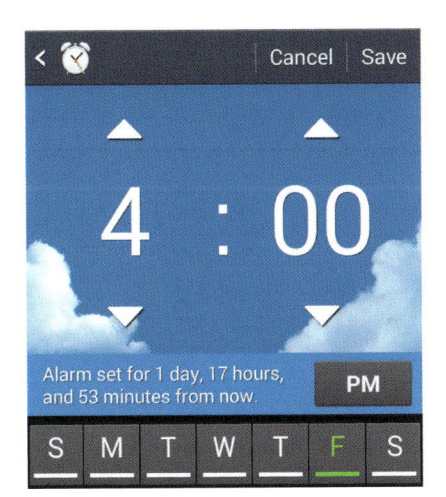

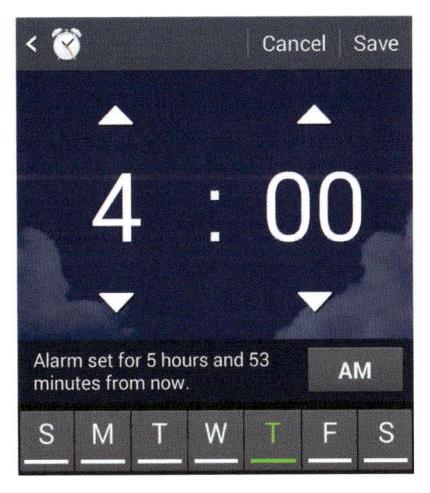

FIGURE 3-90 Should you be confident in this alarm? The settings on the left are clearly wrong, but are you confident with the ones on the right?

Best additional ways to evaluate explorability

Usability studies are a great way to evaluate explorability. I recommend putting extra emphasis on navigation confusion (clue: frequent use of Back), abandon tasks (clue: frequent use of Cancel), or lost work. For explicit save, users clearly don't understand the model if they make changes without saving them. For instant commit, frequent use of Revert suggests that explicit save might be a better commit model.

Is this intuitive?

Let's apply the Eight Attributes of Intuitive UI to some design examples. For each, ask yourself if the design is intuitive, and if not, explain why in terms of the eight attributes. You can compare your answers with mine at the end of this chapter.

Example 1:

Is this intuitive? A digital shower controller from an upscale American hotel (where temperature is measured in Fahrenheit not Celsius!)

Example 2:

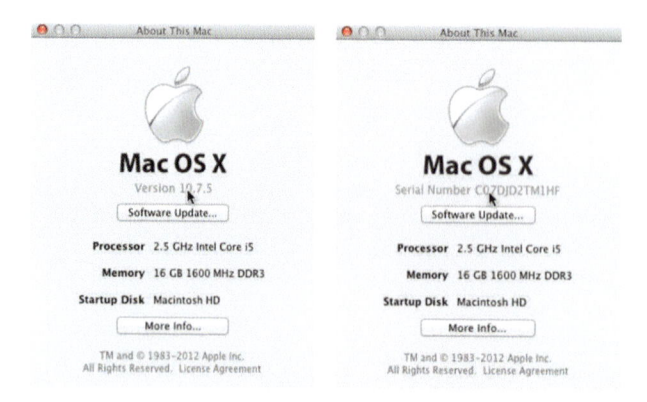

Is this intuitive? Clicking the version number reveals the serial number.

Chapter 3   The Eight Attributes of Intuitive UI

Example 3:

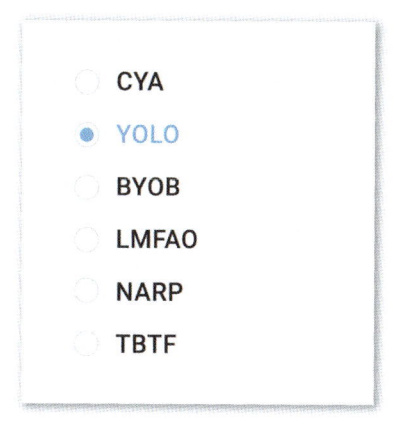

- CYA
- ● YOLO
- BYOB
- LMFAO
- NARP
- TBTF

Is this intuitive? While these security options are clearly made up, this is what they look like to most users.

Example 4:

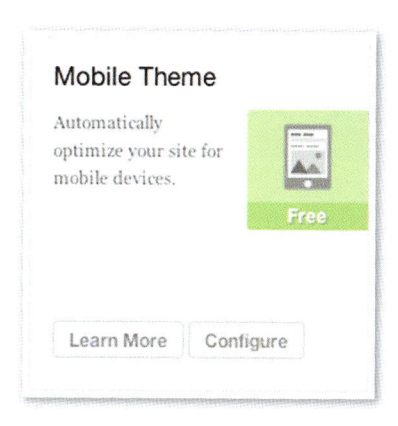

Is this intuitive? Guess how you deactivate this WordPress plugin.

Example 5:

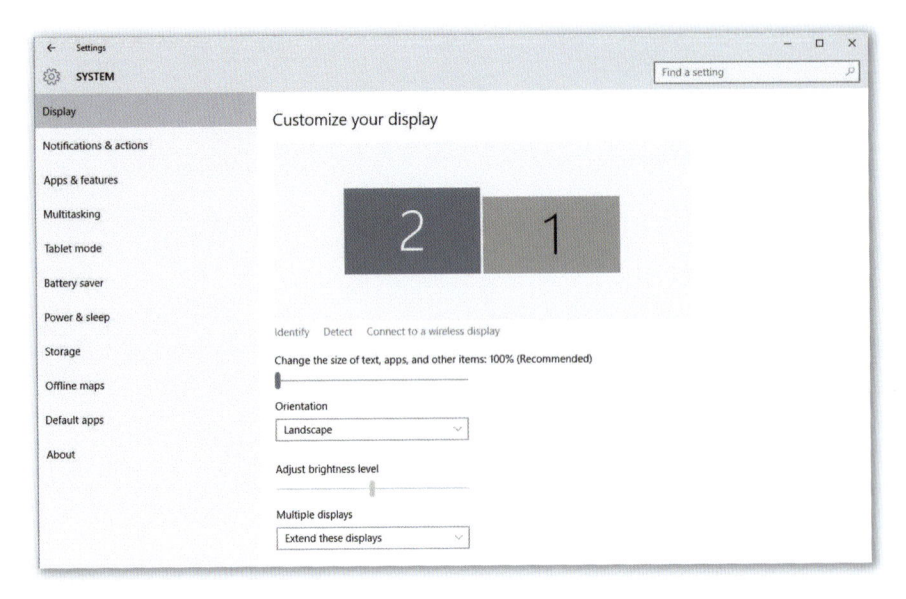

Is this intuitive? Hint: any monitor configuration changes are applied immediately.

Before continuing: I want to reiterate that an unintuitive UI is not necessarily a poor design. For example, shortcuts are usually unintuitive by design as they lack discoverability and affordance. We will explore strategic reasons for unintuitive designs in Chapter 5.

Building an intuitive UI

Let's now apply the Eight Attributes of Intuitive UI to build an intuitive interaction from the ground up with the following design challenge:

> *Design an intuitive, resizable search box for people, companies, or groups, or any specific category—for a page whose primary purpose is not to find things. Most searches are 30 characters or less. Target users might not know exactly what they are looking for, but they often repeat searches.*

This is a familiar design pattern, and it illustrates how all the visual and interactive elements work together and how to justify every design decision based on the Eight Attributes of Intuitive UI.

Let's start with the simplest, unintuitive UI, which would be to have Search hidden behind a hamburger menu:

FIGURE 3-91 Putting Search in a hamburger menu isn't *discoverable*.

This design lacks discoverability. To make the feature discoverable, we should put Search directly on the screen. If the primary purpose of the page were to find things, the search box would go prominently in the top center, but because search is secondary the upper right would be a better choice.

Search needs a text box. For affordance, the dark-gray bordered box plus a flashing caret on focus indicates that the text is editable. The width of the text box indicates the size of the expected input—in this case 30 characters.

FIGURE 3-92 Putting search in upper right makes it *discoverable*. The text box border, caret, and width are *affordances* for editable text and length of expected input.

As is, the user would have to type Enter to perform a search. To make the Search command itself discoverable, it needs a Search button. The button should be placed at the right of the search text box to make the relationship between the two controls predictable (because the flow matches reading order). Applying *Everett's Rule for Custom Icons*, we can safely use the standard search icon here.

FIGURE 3-93 Adding a search command button with the standard search icon for *discoverability*, *affordance*, and *comprehensibility*.

This search box is resizable, so we need to add a resize grabber for discoverability and affordance. On hover or tap, the pointer changes to reinforce both, plus indicates the direction of resize.

FIGURE 3-94 Adding a resizable grabber for *affordance*.

Once the user taps the Search button, the interaction needs to provide responsive feedback. There are a couple of possible solutions: If the app is designed to return search results immediately,

Building an intuitive UI **85**

just start to display them. This is the best solution, and this is what made Google search famous. Another solution would be to display an activity indicator, either where the search results will be displayed or in the Search box itself.

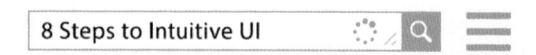

FIGURE 3-95 An activity indicator for *responsive feedback*. Immediately returning results would be better.

With the basic search mechanics done, let's now focus on making the search functionality obvious. Being able to search for people, companies, or groups is not obvious from context, so let's add a placeholder to the text box to make that clear.

FIGURE 3-96 Adding the "Search for people, companies, groups" placeholder for *comprehensibility* and *predictability*.

Target users might not know exactly what they are looking for. For example, suppose the user is looking for someone named Elizabeth Smith. Should the user search for Elizabeth...or Beth, Lisa, Liz, Liza, Eliza, Betty, Bettie, Betsy, or Lisbeth? Would an intuitive UI return no matches for Elizabeth Smith when there are matches for Liz Smith? If we are designing a tool to help users find people, shouldn't the design actually *help* users find people? Of course it should, because intuitive UIs are efficient.

FIGURE 3-97 *Efficient* search returns results based on users' intent, not their literal input.

On occasion, users might search for a name and get the wrong type of results. For example, let's assume that the name *Everett McKay* is extremely common (work with me here), with thousands of people and dozens of companies having that name. For efficiency, users might want to search for a specific category. While we could attempt to use just custom icons for this purpose, let's apply *Everett's Rule for Custom Icons* and use icon+text label pairs instead.

FIGURE 3-98 An *efficient* search for specific categories.

Users repeat searches, so for efficiency let's facilitate repeats.

FIGURE 3-99 Adding a most-recently-used drop-down for *efficient* repeated searches.

But once users start typing, they are indicating more specific intent. For efficiency, let's adjust the content of the drop-down to show still-relevant recent searches, plus make relevant suggestions.

FIGURE 3-100 Adjusting the most-recently-used drop-down based on user input for *efficient* repeated searches.

Finally, users often make small mistakes, so what if users type a search that was close but not quite? They should be able to change the search and try again, rather than completely start over. But surprisingly, some search UIs immediately clear themselves or don't allow for modification—very unforgiving. Instead, we can let users decide when to clear by providing a clear command in the text box.

FIGURE 3-101 Our final design: adding a Clear command for *forgiveness* and *efficiency*.

Instead of applying this process, we could have just chosen the standard search box pattern.

Building an intuitive UI   **87**

FIGURE 3-102 The standard search box pattern, without applying the Eight Attributes of Intuitive UI.

But the results would not be intuitive. Users would have to think, experiment, and deduce how the interaction works because this design makes no effort to be self-explanatory. **Applying the Eight Attributes of Intuitive UI helps you get the details right and defend and prioritize those design details to your team.**

Summary

The definition of intuitive UI helps us determine whether a UI design is intuitive, and the Eight Attributes of Intuitive UI help us make a design intuitive. These attributes are based on the interaction lifecycle, which are the steps users typically go through to achieve a goal. Use these attributes to make design decisions, identify design problems, and persuade others—better and more efficiently. Doing so will give you an objective, principled understanding of what makes a UI intuitive. It's not a matter of opinion.

Remember that having an unintuitive UI doesn't necessarily mean that your app is poorly designed. It might be highly usable for motivated, trained users. Many successful products have unintuitive UIs—sometimes deliberately—as you'll see in Chapter 5. What it means instead: if applying the Eight Attributes of Intuitive UI reveals problems, your app will be more intuitive if you correct them. **Apply this chapter in good spirit—to help you appreciate what's good about your app, and identify opportunities to make it even better.**

Exercises

Apply what you have learned in this chapter with the following exercises:

1. Find an example UI that you believe is unintuitive. Try to convince someone else that it is unintuitive based on the Eight Attributes of Intuitive UI. Were you able to make your case?

2. For the unintuitive UI in Exercise 1, apply the Eight Attributes of Intuitive UI to redesign it. Try to convince the same person that the new design is intuitive.

3. Find an example UI that has the Eight Attributes of Intuitive UI but lacks consistency with similar designs such that the results are unintuitive. Which steps in the interaction lifecycle were a problem?

4. For each of the Eight Attributes of Intuitive UI, find an example that does a great job of implementing the attribute.

5. For each of the Eight Attributes of Intuitive UI, find an example that fails to implement the attribute. For each, recommend a design change to fix the problem.

6. Find two designs that have the intuitive attributes but their poor execution makes them unintuitive anyway. An example might be a control that has a misleading affordance.

7. Think of an interaction that you discovered only after a significant period of time after initially using the product (for days or even months). What design detail specifically required so much time?

8. For the Inflight Entertainment controller shown below, redesign the controller to eliminate the need for any instructions.

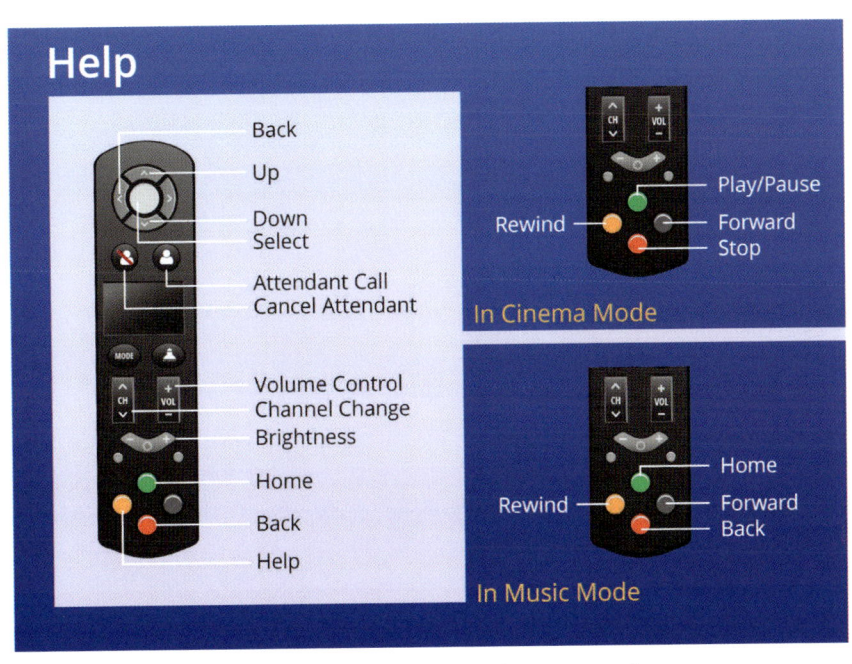

FIGURE 3-103 The instructions for an Inflight Entertainment controller.

9. Apply the Eight Attributes of Intuitive UI to voice-driven interfaces. Which attributes don't or can't apply? Which attributes need to be enhanced to compensate? Work through a specific task for both touch-based and voice-based UI, and compare.

10. Apply the Eight Attributes of Intuitive UI to command-line interfaces. Which attributes don't or can't apply? Which attributes need to be enhanced to compensate? Work through a specific task for both command line UI and graphical UI, and compare.

Exercises 89

My answers

EXAMPLE 1: The On/Off and Hot/Cold labels describe the effect of the controls, but the Push and Hold label indicates the interaction. The need for push and hold is unexpected as the affordance of a push button suggests the need for only a simple push. Note that the hotel had to add this label later, after they discovered (likely immediately) that the controller wasn't intuitive.

EXAMPLE 2: Clicking the version number to review the serial number is unintuitive because there is no discoverability, no click affordance, and no expectation of this result. That said, this isn't necessarily a problem as this is a shortcut for expert users only. Nonexperts can get the same information by clicking More Info...

EXAMPLE 3: These clearly fake security options are unintuitive because the labels aren't comprehensible. I'm assuming the target users aren't security experts. It would be intuitive to use terms like DNS, DHCP, and QOS for advanced settings targeted at network experts, but not for ordinary users. This pattern is common—many UIs present options for which target users can't make informed decisions without consulting documentation.

EXAMPLE 4: While you would naturally assume that you could deactivate by clicking Configure, you in fact have to click Learn More, which reveals a Deactivate command. This design is unintuitive because of poor discoverability; Learn More suggests help-related content only. Some people have suggested that this design might be a *dark pattern* to discourage deactivation. My guess is that these plugin control panels allow for only two buttons, so the developer multiplexed the button function as a work-around.

EXAMPLE 5: The hint was misleading, which reveals the problem. Any monitor configuration changes *appear* to be applied immediately, but in fact they are not. This page uses explicit commit, but unfortunately the Apply button is "below the fold." Thus, there is misleading feedback (the feedback suggests instant commit), poor discoverability (Apply button below the fold), and explorability problems (confusing commit models). Possible solutions: use instant commit (with a Revert button to undo changes) or make sure that the Apply button is always visible.

Talk about unforgiving—and unsafe defaults!

'Friendly Fire' Deaths Traced to Dead Battery

https://www.washingtonpost.com/archive/politics/2002/03/24/friendly-fire-deaths-traced-to-dead-battery

March 24, 2002

The deadliest "friendly fire" incident of the war in Afghanistan was triggered in December by the simple act of a U.S. Special Forces air controller changing the battery on a Global Positioning System device he was using to target a Taliban outpost north of Kandahar, a senior defense official said yesterday.

Three Special Forces soldiers were killed and 20 were injured when a 2,000-pound, satellite-guided bomb landed, not on the Taliban outpost, but on a battalion command post occupied by American forces and a group of Afghan allies, including Hamid Karzai, now the interim prime minister.

The U.S. Central Command, which runs the Afghan war, has never explained how the coordinates got mixed up or who was responsible for relaying the U.S. position to a B-52 bomber, which fired a
Joint Direct Attack Munition (JDAM) at the Americans.

But the senior defense official explained yesterday that the Air Force combat controller was using a Precision Lightweight GPS Receiver, known to soldiers as a "plugger," to calculate the Taliban's coordinates for a B-52 attack. The controller did not realize that after he changed the device's battery, the machine was programmed to automatically come back on displaying coordinates for its own location, the official said.

Minutes before the fatal B-52 strike, which also killed five Afghan opposition soldiers and injured 18 others, the controller had used the GPS receiver to calculate the latitude and longitude of the Taliban position in minutes and seconds for an airstrike by a Navy F/A-18, the official said.

Then, with the B-52 approaching the target, the air controller did a second calculation in "degree decimals" required by the bomber crew. The controller had performed the calculation and recorded the position, the official said, when the receiver battery died.

Without realizing the machine was programmed to come back on showing the coordinates of its own location, the controller mistakenly called in the American position to the B-52. The JDAM landed with devastating precision.

CHAPTER 4

Bonus intuitive UI attributes

Less is more, right?

One of my goals for this book is to make understanding intuitive UI design as simple as possible, so I chose the Eight Attributes of Intuitive UI defined in Chapter 3 to be minimal yet complete. Doing so makes them easier to remember and apply. The interaction lifecycle is an excellent tool for structuring a minimal, complete set of primary attributes. After all, if target users can get through all the steps in the interaction lifecycle without reasoning, experimenting, etc., it stands to reason that the design must be intuitive. Any design reasoning beyond that is a bonus.

In this chapter, I'll describe several attributes that affect intuitiveness but in indirect or redundant ways. They include *familiar* **and** *learnable*, **which many people consider synonyms for** *intuitive*. There's no harm in considering these attributes when making design decisions, but there is usually no harm in skipping them either.

Consider this chapter optional if you're in a hurry. It's a worthwhile read if you want a full command of the intuitive UI vocabulary—which can be especially important when you are trying to persuade managers, stakeholders, and clients about design decisions. **You should read this chapter if people on your team believe that intuitive apps are familiar, consistent, and learnable—and nothing more. A better understanding of these bonus attributes will help you better explain why the Eight Attributes of Intuitive UI are the ones that matter most.**

Familiar

As I mentioned in the Preface, **when I started my research on intuitive UI, the only UX book in my substantial library to define this term was Jef Raskin's** *The Humane Interface*, **where Raskin defines** *intuitive* **to mean** *familiar*.

> One of the most laudatory terms used to describe an interface is to say that it is "intuitive." When examined closely, this concept turns out to vanish like a pea in a shell game and be replaced with the more ordinary but accurate term "familiar."

Raskin implies that *familiar* is more meaningful than *intuitive*, but I disagree because *familiar* is neither necessary nor sufficient. Let's define *familiar* as an assessment of whether target users can apply previously learned knowledge to the current interaction, and let's explore a few examples.

We'll start with light switches—what UI could be more familiar?

FIGURE 4-1 A common light switch configuration.

Light switches are very familiar, but are they intuitive? If they were, you should be able to accurately predict the result of flipping the switches. Before you answer, let me give you a hint—suppose these switches are in a hotel bathroom. Another hint: the leftmost switch turns on the bathroom fan. Not intuitive, right? And if you're like me, you have discovered this problem by taking a shower and then, afterward, realizing there was a fan you were supposed to turn on first.

Now consider this alternative design:

Adding an explicit "Fan" label makes the design more discoverable, comprehensible, and predictable, and therefore more intuitive. But labeled light switches are rare so arguably less familiar. Familiarity alone doesn't help—in fact, familiarity misleads us into thinking the left switch controls a light instead of a fan (hence the name "light switch" in lieu of the more accurate "switch").

FIGURE 4-2 A less common, more intuitive light switch configuration with an explicit "Fan" label.

94   Chapter 4   Bonus intuitive UI attributes

When a UI element's intuitive attributes are misleading or conflicting, familiarity is more likely to confuse than clarify. That's why "If it looks the same, it should behave the same" is a frequently cited design principle.

All this said, familiarity is important and helpful—as a secondary attribute. Familiarity allows us to immediately recognize these as light switches, understand their interaction, and set our expectations. But familiarity alone doesn't give us any information about the purpose of each individual switch, so when the switches are unlabeled we must determine their effect through experimentation.

Let's look at another example, which will be familiar to readers of Don Norman's *The Design of Everyday Things*. **Norman points out that doors are confusing when their handles have misleading affordances.** Such doors are referred to as *Norman doors*. What interaction could be more familiar than opening doors? Yet familiarity doesn't save these confusing designs. I believe Norman's book could be accurately retitled *How Familiar, Everyday Things Can Be Confusing and Unintuitive*. The point being that familiarity and intuitiveness often don't correlate.

FIGURE 4-3 Although very familiar, door handles can be unintuitive. The need for a label is a clue there's a problem. Note that the handle's design says pull but the label says push.

Let's look at one more example. **I like to evaluate interfaces that were clearly not designed for me. I try to see how much I can figure out even though I'm not the target user. Give that a try with this helicopter control panel shown in Figure 4-6.**

FIGURE 4-4 The vertical speed gauge.

FIGURE 4-5 The direction compass.

FIGURE 4-6 A control panel from a Robinson R44 helicopter.

How much were you able to figure out? When I tried this, I figured out the gauge shown in Figure 4-4 right away.

Given the context, the labeling, and natural mapping, **it is immediately clear that this gauge indicates whether the helicopter is ascending or descending, and how rapidly. By contrast, the gauge shown in Figure 4-5 was more difficult to understand.**

What is 21…24…W… **Oh, it's the compass, which—with the possible exception of the fuel gauge—is the most familiar control in the cockpit!** Even though this is familiar, its presentation isn't immediately recognizable. Familiar purpose, but unfamiliar presentation.

96 Chapter 4 Bonus intuitive UI attributes

With these examples, I hope you see the problem. **If we equate intuitive with familiar and decide that a specific UI element is familiar and therefore intuitive, we can easily be misled. The Eight Attributes of Intuitive UI are a much better indicator.** Take a look again: the vertical speed gauge is intuitive not because it's familiar but because it has the right design attributes.

Tweet This!

> *Familiarity is a secondary attribute that affects discoverability, affordance, comprehensibility, and predictability. When poorly designed, familiar UIs are likely to confuse or mislead because they set incorrect expectations.*

Consistent

Consistency is a much better intuitive attribute than *familiarity* because it's more specific and easier to evaluate. Let's define *consistency* as conformity of appearance and behavior within an application or across applications. Good consistency helps make UIs easier to use and more intuitive by leveraging existing knowledge and making interactions more discoverable and predictable.

Contrary to its dictionary definition, intuitive UIs are not about instinct, not about knowledge and behavior that we're born with. Rather, **intuitive UIs leverage users' existing knowledge from prior experience and the context they are in.**

But where do users get that prior knowledge? It could be based on domain knowledge. It could also be based on prior experience with your app—things your users have learned with the current version or even prior versions. **An important perspective is based on Jakob Nielsen's *Law of the Internet User Experience*, which I have taken the liberty to generalize to the following:**

> *Users spend most of their time using software other than yours.*

This simple observation is quite profound. **Your users' understanding of where to discover features; how to interpret affordances, labels, and icons; and how to predict outcomes accurately is based on their prior experience with all other software.** If your app is inconsistent with your target users' prior experiences, it's your app that is unintuitive. Reassigning a standard shortcut or gesture might seem sensible to you, but the lack of consistency will confuse your users.

Surprisingly, this means that we can have designs that are clearly missing intuitive attributes (like discoverability and affordance), but target users will still consider them to be intuitive based on conventions/idioms they have learned with other apps.

Let's consider some common idioms: interactive logos in the upper-left corner of a page (to go Home) and interactive item headings and images on a summary page (to go to the item's page).

Experienced users will know to tap these without hesitation. Still, it's wise to use them as shortcuts and have discoverable alternatives with clear affordances (such as an explicit Home command).

FIGURE 4-7 Interactive logos, headings, and images. They don't have interactive affordances, but experienced users will know to tap them.

The opposite is also true: designs that include the eight intuitive attributes can fail to be intuitive because users are misled based on their expectations of consistency. If a design looks familiar, users assume they know how it works and they likely won't examine it carefully.

My favorite example: the remote control for my Panasonic TV. Review this design and see if you can spot the problem; then compare your answer to mine at the end of the chapter. Hint: I don't expect everything on a TV remote to be fully intuitive, but there are certain common functions that I expect to be.

If it looks like a duck and is located like a duck, users will assume it's a duck—even if clearly labeled to the contrary.

Example 1:

Is this intuitive? My Panasonic TV remote control.

FIGURE 4-8 An unintuitive non-duck. If your duck needs a label, its design is probably faulty.

98   Chapter 4   Bonus intuitive UI attributes

In the next figure, the unintuitive duck is a standard list search box, which is not where it first appears to be.

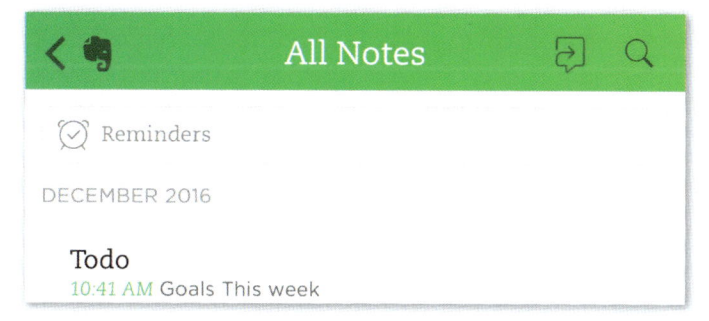

FIGURE 4-9 The label clearly indicates Reminders, but it has the location of a standard search box. Guess where I go when I want to search my notes?

Possibly the best example of poor consistency is the red LED status indicators found in many electronic devices (another extremely familiar UI). **Generally, what does a red LED mean? The surprising answer: it means some kind of status. Red LEDs are used so inconsistently that they can mean just about anything,** from device on to device off (but plugged in), from success to failure.

FIGURE 4-10 From left to right, these red LEDs mean on, off, success, failure, low battery, charging, fully charged.

The only reason red LED status indicators work is that users can figure out their meaning from context or perhaps quick experimentation. Simply adding a label removes confusion.

FIGURE 4-11 Labels help eliminate confusion!

With the glaring exception of red LEDs status indicators, **the use of red, yellow, and green as status colors is an excellent example of consistency.** The interpretation of color is culturally dependent. Red, for example, is interpreted as danger in western cultures but as auspicious good luck in eastern cultures. **As I mentioned in Chapter 3, because the meaning of status colors was established globally by the United Nations *Conventions on Road Signs and Signals*, you don't have to localize them.** Regardless of the cultural connotations in China, a red traffic light still means stop in Beijing.

Consistent   **99**

A great way to achieve consistency is to make sure your team is familiar with your app's platform guidelines. For iOS, check the *iOS Human Interface Guidelines*, and for Android, check both the *Android Design Principles* and *Material Design Guidelines*.

All this said, it's important to distinguish between good consistency (which improves usability) and bad consistency (which harms usability). Often bad consistency is justified only for the sake of consistency itself and no other reason.

FIGURE 4-12 Stop! And good luck!

Tweet This!

I have seen many examples of bad consistency over the years—it's a very easy trap to fall into. When in doubt, a simple question to ask is, "What does this consistency accomplish?" If the only answer you can give is "Consistency!" your design might be better off without it.

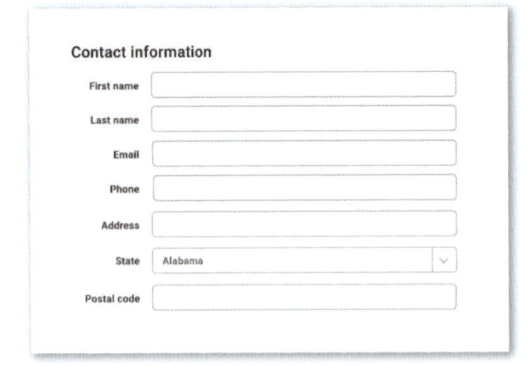

FIGURE 4-13 Making all the fields a uniform length doesn't make this form easier to use or understand. Rather, it makes it harder to scan or understand the size of the expected input. The version on the right is better.

Consistency is a secondary attribute that affects discoverability, affordance, comprehensibility, predictability. But watch out for bad consistency.

Learnable

Many people believe that intuitive UIs are easily learnable. On occasion, you might hear someone assert that a product is "intuitive once you learn how to use it." Surprisingly, this is wrong! As you'll see in Chapter 5, an easily learnable UI can be described as highly usable, **but the goal of an intuitive UI is to avoid the need for learning in the first place—making learnability merely a consolation prize.** (So, saying a product is "very usable once you learn it" is a more credible claim.)

Interactions that require learning are often that way because they are poorly designed and users must learn to overcome design flaws. (Catastrophic and embarrassing outcomes are, unintentionally, a particularly effective learning tool.) If you discover that your design requires learning, try to find a simple alternative that eliminates the need. Often, you can.

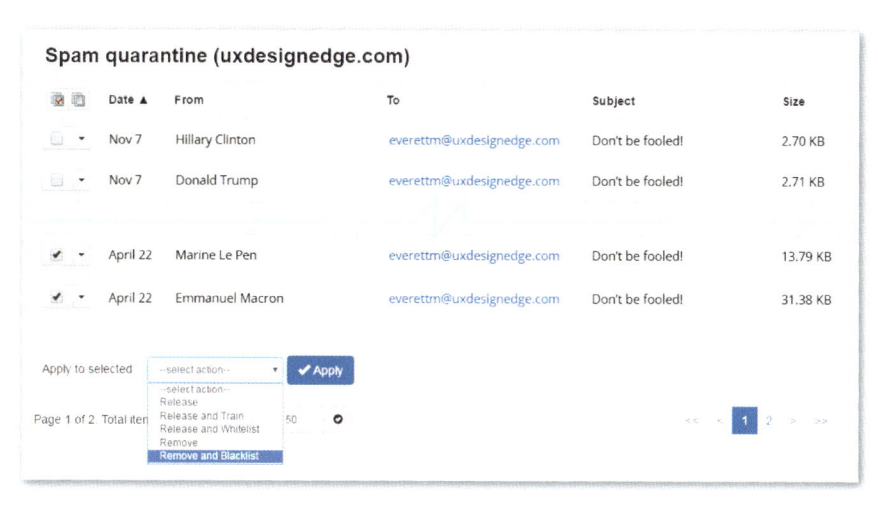

FIGURE 4-14 When using this list, I have learned to start by checking all the items at the top before scrolling—to work around a design flaw. The flaw: I don't have easy access to what I need when I need it. The bulk selection is at the top of the list whereas the bulk selection commands are at the bottom.

Let's work through a familiar example: a shower controller. I recently stayed at a hotel in Europe that used the shower controller shown in Figure 4-15. I travel a lot, but I find European shower controllers are exotic compared to what you typically find in North America.

The first morning, I looked at the controller and noticed that the indicator suggests I should rotate the top knob left to turn on the shower. I did so and it worked as expected. The second morning? I looked at the controller and noticed that the indicator suggests I should rotate the top knob left to turn on the shower, which I immediately did. The third morning? Same thing.

But what did I learn? Nothing! I didn't have to learn anything because the design is intuitive. In effect, I *relearned* how to use the shower controller each morning, but I didn't retain the information nor did I need to. If I had to memorize or experiment, that would reveal a design flaw.

This is exactly as it should be—if a design has the appropriate attributes of intuitive UI, there is no need to learn anything. Learnability is required only when any important intuitive attributes are missing. Remove the legend, for example, and I would have to learn how to use the shower controller through experimentation and memorization.

FIGURE 4-15 A hotel shower controller.

A general observation from long-term usability studies is that users learn far less about our apps than we assume. A simple way to verify this would be to ask users to list everything they have learned about your app from memory—unaided by the app itself. Unless they use it daily, expect to receive a surprisingly short list.

As we'll see in Chapter 5, some interactions are unintuitive by design, making learnability important. For example, shortcuts and gestures must be learned because they lack discoverability and affordance. For such interactions, learnability is very important and attributes like consistency, conventions, mnemonics, and natural mapping go a long way.

While important, learnability applies more to not quite intuitive design than to intuitive design. For most interactions, your design goal should be to eliminate the need for learning in the first place.

Learnable is a secondary attribute that compensates for when any of the Eight Attributes of Intuitive UI are missing. Learnability isn't the goal; it's a consolation prize.

Invisible

Many people describe intuitive UIs as *invisible*. This is true, but only if we define "invisible" properly. Intuitive UIs enable users to be fully immersed in their work instead of the interface itself, which leads to what Mihály Csíkszentmihályi famously refers to as flow. This is also what Steve Krug is referring to with *Don't Make Me Think*. Poorly designed UIs require thought, and invisible here means that users aren't thinking about the UI. **We are not using "invisible" literally—whether users actually see anything on the screen is beside the point.** (In this sense, a poorly designed voice-based interface could be very "visible" if it's distracting.)

While we can regard being invisible as a secondary attribute, it is vague at best and misleading at worst. I can't imagine a team having a meaningful design discussion in which decisions are made based on a design being more or less invisible or resulting in more or less flow. That discussion would be a long, hard road to difficult consensus and poor decisions. But all too often, invisible UI is interpreted as "the best UI is no UI"—this interpretation is very wrong.

Tweet This!

Instead of trying to correctly interpret *invisible* **or worrying about flow, focus on the Eight Attributes of Intuitive UI.** If making a UI "invisible" enhances those attributes (by doing the right thing automatically, for example), embrace it. But if making a UI "invisible" harms those attributes (for example, by adversely affecting discoverability, affordance, or feedback), reject it.

Let's work through an example. **People often assert that "the best error message is no error message"; error messages are seen as the ultimate visible flow stoppers.** As are other messages like warnings and confirmations. These are plausible assertions if our goal is invisible flow. But is this true? It's certainly true for routine confirmations.

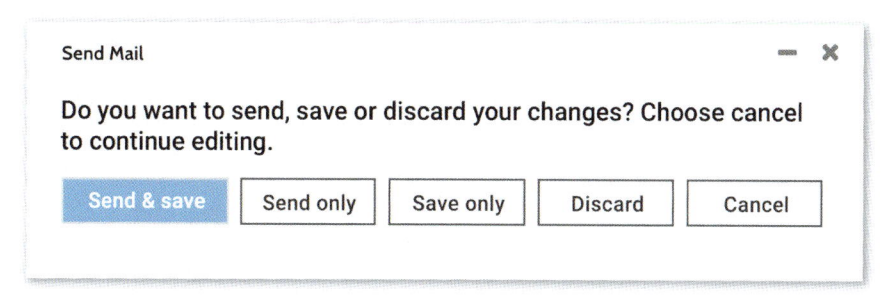

FIGURE 4-16 A flow stopper.

Confirmations, by their very nature, are flow stoppers. The user just gave a command saying, "I want to do this" and the confirmation stops the user to ask, "Are you sure you want to do this?" Of course, the answer is yes—often with a groan.

But properly designed confirmations give users a good reason not to proceed, instead of routine "double checking." A good confirmation forces users to stop and think—by design. And if there is a good reason not to proceed, the confirming step is intuitive and doesn't unnecessarily harm flow. American Airlines Flight 965 to Cali Colombia tragically crashed into a mountain due to "pilot error," specifically because a pilot incorrectly programmed the flight system. A good confirmation might have helped prevent this disaster.

Invisible   **103**

FIGURE 4-17 Also a flow stopper, but rightly so and still intuitive. Yes, sometimes you must make the user think!

Invisible and flow are secondary attributes that, while important, are vague and easily misinterpreted.

Being intuitive in stressful situations

The Eight Attributes of Intuitive UI have an implicit assumption that isn't always true: that the user is fully composed and not in a stressful situation. That isn't necessarily the case—some tasks occur in high-stress situations. Even without stress, users need sufficient time to understand what they are being asked to do before responding.

Perhaps the worst offenders here are UIs that are displayed automatically (due to specific circumstances) and then immediately removed before the user has a chance to review and interact. Unless the user has requested some long-running task, assume that the user will continue to interact with the app and that doing so might remove the UI.

Consider the problem of signing into Wi-Fi in iOS. Once you choose a Wi-Fi hotspot, you might also have to sign in. iOS kindly displays a sign-in screen but then immediately removes it if you were in the middle of an interaction—with no easy, obvious way to get it back.

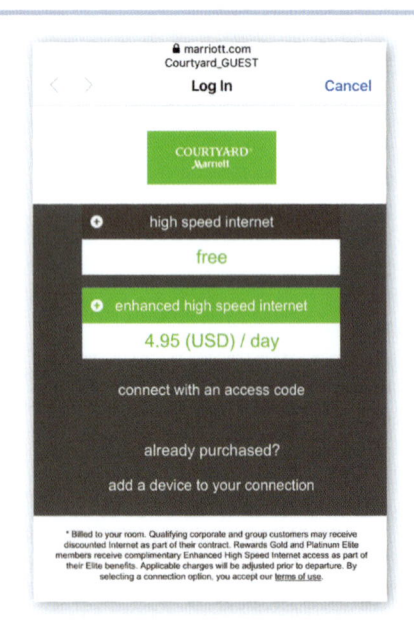

FIGURE 4-18 Signing into a Wi-Fi hotspot using iOS. Now you see it, now you don't!

104   Chapter 4   Bonus intuitive UI attributes

An intuitive UI gives users sufficient time to understand what is going on, plus sufficient time to respond, along with an easily discoverable way to restore the UI if dismissed accidentally.

Another prime offender is the unnecessarily short task timeout. Want your users to panic and make more mistakes when purchasing a product? Give them an unnecessary two-minute time out.

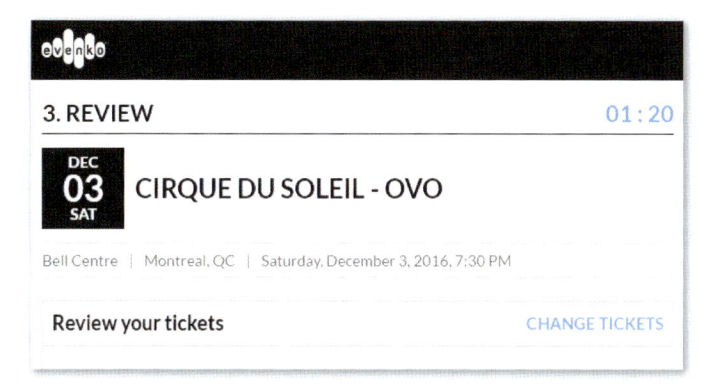

FIGURE 4-19 Where's my credit card? Only 80 seconds left... Hope I have my wallet nearby.

Two minutes to provide a credit card? **Now I'm worried that the task will time out and I'll have to start completely over. That's unforgiving!**

Even routine interactions like pressing a Record button can be unintuitive when users are in stressful situations and their attention lies elsewhere.

FIGURE 4-20 I'm recording my daughter's award ceremony. But crap! Tapping the Record button didn't take effect and I didn't even notice because I was focused on the ceremony. I didn't record anything!

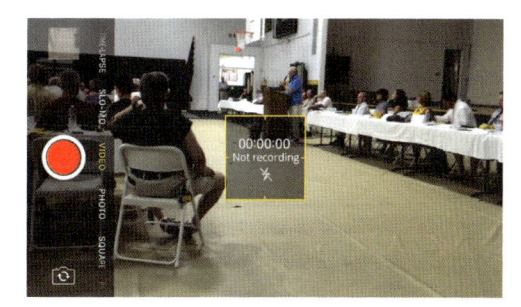

FIGURE 4-21 With this redesign, there's no question whether I'm recording.

Stress-free interaction is a secondary attribute that affects predictability, efficiency, and forgiveness. Even routine interactions can be unintuitive in high-stress situations.

Digestible

And for the fun of it, let's explore one more bonus attribute: *digestible*. **People occasionally describe an intuitive UI as easily digestible. But what exactly does that mean?** Literally, it means that it can be consumed and eventually pooped out. Hopefully, what digestible is really supposed to mean is easily *comprehensible*, which of course is one of the Eight Attributes of Intuitive UI, or perhaps *scannable*.

Tweet This!

UX professionals use too many vague, abstract terms or metaphors to describe design concepts. Because such language lacks practical, specific meaning, these terms and metaphors make it difficult to communicate your ideas persuasively to your team. Everyone needs to interpret what these metaphors mean, perhaps differently.

It's surprising how much impact a meaningful vocabulary can make. If you tell me my UI isn't digestible, I have no idea what that means or what to do about it. But if you tell me a UI element isn't discoverable, has a misleading affordance, or has a label that isn't comprehensible, I know exactly what that means and I know what to do about it. **The discussion transforms from being personal and subjective to being objective and actionable.** That's a big, big deal!

Let's ditch the metaphors too!

Try to get your team to use more meaningful language during design decisions. Explain why it is important with some good examples. If someone describes a UI as being digestible (or smooth, frictionless, or natural), ask "What exactly does that mean?" or suggest a more specific, meaningful term, as with "By digestible do you mean comprehensible?" The sooner you get rid of that vague language and questionable metaphors, the sooner your team will have more productive design discussions. **You will be pleasantly surprised by the difference!**

> *Have design discussions using a specific, meaningful vocabulary. It's very difficult to have productive discussions based on vague, abstract terms and metaphors. When appropriate, ask team members to define the terms or propose alternative language.*

Summary

I chose the Eight Attributes of Intuitive UI to be minimal yet complete—and therefore easier and more practical to apply. *Familiar*, *consistent*, *learnable*, *invisible*, and *digestible* are often considered attributes too. While they do affect intuitiveness, they do so indirectly or redundantly, so there is usually no harm in skipping them.

Exercises

Apply what you have learned in this chapter with the following exercises:

1. Find an example UI that you believe is intuitive. Try to convince someone that it is intuitive by focusing on *familiarity*, *consistency*, *invisibility*, and *learnability*. Were you able to make your case?

2. Repeat the previous exercise for a UI that is unintuitive.

3. Find another example UI that you believe is intuitive. Try to convince someone else that it is intuitive by focusing on the Eight Attributes of Intuitive UI from Chapter 3. Were you able to make your case? Compare your results here with those for Exercise 1.

4. Repeat the previous exercise for a UI that is unintuitive. Compare your results here with those for Exercise 2.

5. Consider an app that you have learned quite well and make a list, from memory, of everything you have learned. Review the list and characterize each item. Did you learn a lot or a little? How many of the things you learned could have been eliminated through better design?

6. Choose a popular app that you believe is intuitive. Ask several people who are familiar with the app to (independently) list everything they have learned about using the app—without looking at it. How long are those lists? What are the common items in the lists? Based on the results, do you think the app is learnable? Did this exercise demonstrate that *learnability* is important?

7. Make a list of common situations where beeping is used as feedback. Design the sonic attributes of each beep (pitch, dissonance, loudness, rhythm) to match the specific feedback, yet be clearly distinct from the others. Assess your results. Are there situations for which beeps are poor feedback?

8. Find example UIs that are visible (that is, the opposite of invisible) and that break your flow. Was breaking your flow justified? Does it harm the intuitiveness of the app?

My answers

EXAMPLE 1: While there are many remote-control commands, as a user I expect the Power, Channel, and Volume controls to be fully intuitive. Nearly every remote control that I am familiar with places the Channel rocker buttons on the right and the Volume rocker on the left (although this might not be true where you live). But not my Panasonic, which reverses the order. The reason this is unintuitive is that we often change channels or the volume without reading the button labels, and the lack of consistency results in errors that we discover through experimentation.

CHAPTER 5

Strategically unintuitive

You really can have too much of a good thing...

Now that you know the definition of intuitive UI plus the Eight Attributes of Intuitive UI, you can put this knowledge to good use by making your interactions intuitive. Your users will love you for it.

But this begs the question: **should everything be intuitive? The surprising answer is *no*! It turns out that it's not practical to make everything intuitive, and some interactions are actually better if they're unintuitive.**

The need for unintuitive UI isn't a rehash of the common excuses we reviewed in Chapter 1. Rather, it's recognizing that **design decisions are ultimately tradeoffs and that other design objectives besides intuitiveness might be more important.** Designing for great performance is a good example. As designers, we need to be aware of these tradeoffs and understand when to make decisions deliberately in favor of designs that aren't fully intuitive—*strategically rather than accidentally*.

Tweet This!

> Design decisions are ultimately tradeoffs, and sometime other factors are more important. It's fine to design interactions that aren't fully intuitive—strategically rather than accidentally.

The cost of intuitive

There is a cost to making a UI intuitive. Most of the time that cost is well worth paying, but sometimes it's not. **Here are some situations where the cost might be too high:**

- **Discoverability**   Designing everything to be discoverable might result in cluttered, complex screens, making it difficult for a user to find what's most important. Discoverability might expose features that are inappropriate for some users or overexpose features or options that are rarely needed.

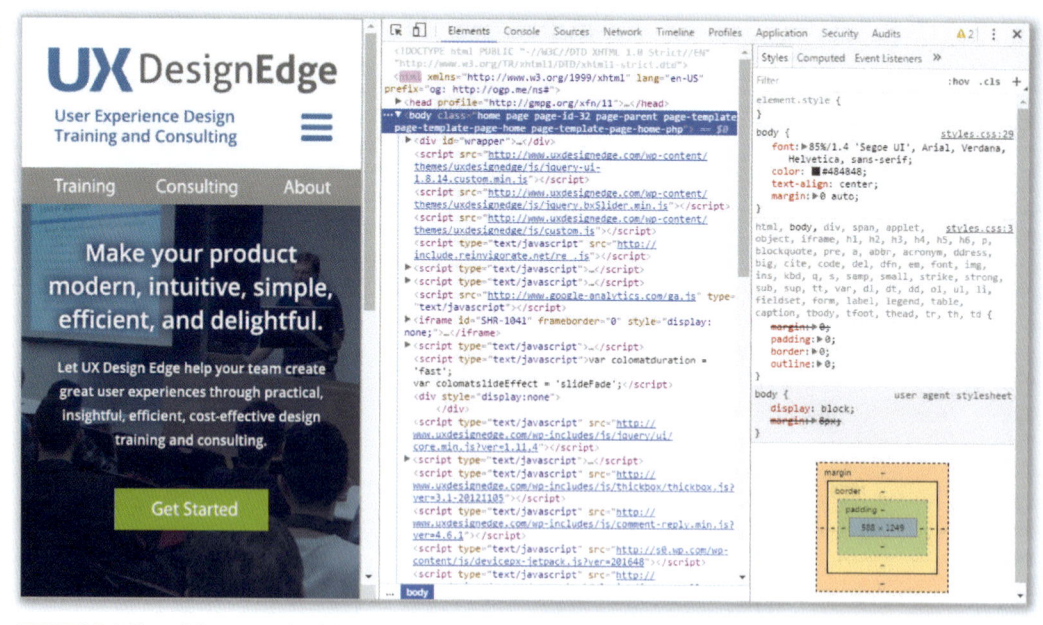

FIGURE 5-1 Not all features should be discoverable. Developer tools are for programmers only, so they should be well hidden from nonprogrammers. The target users will know where to find them.

- **Affordance**   Giving everything a clear affordance might also result in cluttered, heavy screens.

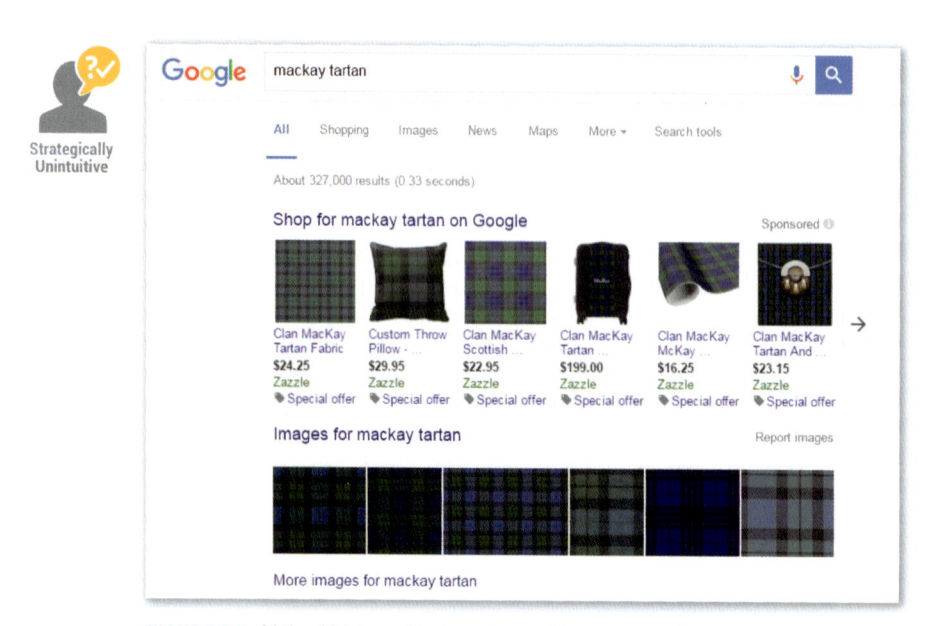

FIGURE 5-2 Of the 40 interactive targets on this screen, only two have a button affordance (Search and the More arrow button). The rest are links, tabs, thumbnails, and a clickable logo. Through convention the link affordance (underlining) isn't necessary.

110   Chapter 5   Strategically unintuitive

- **Comprehensibility and predictability** Making everything comprehensible and predictable might require too much explanation. Sometimes it's better to require a bit of thought or experimentation to fill in the blanks.

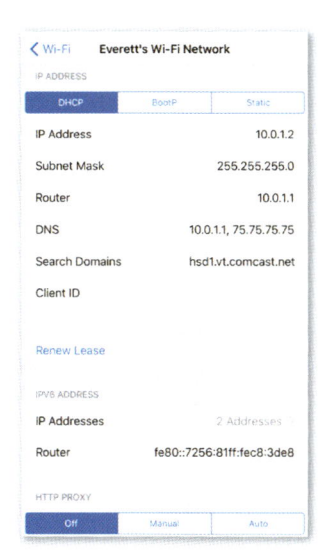

FIGURE 5-3 For advanced network settings, comprehensibility and predictability require too much explanation. The target users of these settings understand what they mean. It's OK that they aren't intuitive for everyone else.

- **Forgiveness** Some interactions require commitment because making them forgiving might not be practical or might harm performance.

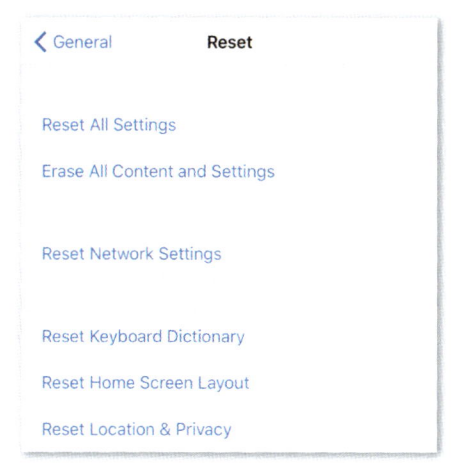

FIGURE 5-4 It's not practical to make everything forgiving. Reset All Settings requires commitment. Don't expect a lot of forgiveness on this screen.

The cost of intuitive   **111**

Beyond these design tradeoffs, making a UI fully intuitive entails development costs. So, while a Minimal Viable Product (MVP) needs discoverability, affordance, comprehensibility, and predictability, perhaps the other intuitive attributes can wait.

The Seven Good Reasons for Unintuitive UI

Based on these costs, there are (at least) seven good reasons to design a UI that isn't fully intuitive:

- **Advanced, infrequent, optional commands** It might not be worth making these interactions discoverable, especially when doing so harms the discoverability of the important, frequently used commands needed by everyone or leads to unnecessary complexity.

FIGURE 5-5 Remote controls are notorious for exposing everything. Most of the time, users just want to turn on and off the TV, change the channel, and adjust the volume.

FIGURE 5-6 Thanks for all the options, but I will go with Start Windows Normally every single time! Better to make those alternatives difficult to discover to simplify the choice that is nearly certain.

Chapter 5 Strategically unintuitive

- **Shortcuts and gestures** With a few exceptions, the nature of shortcuts and gestures is to not have discoverability or affordance. This isn't a problem as long as they are redundant, meaning that they duplicate the functionality of normal (and more discoverable) commands.

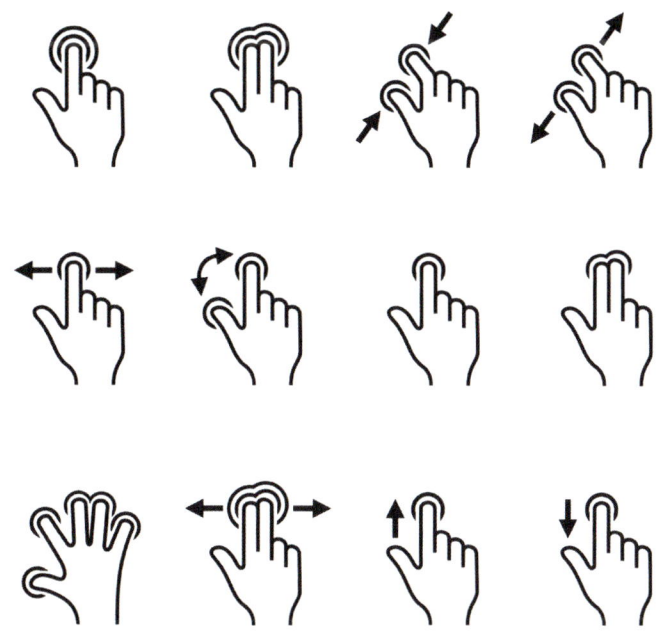

FIGURE 5-7 Good thing all these gestures don't have affordances.

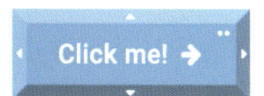

FIGURE 5-8 Is "overaffordanced" even a word?

- **Inevitable discoverability** You don't need discoverability if it's a distraction and there's no way users can *not* find the commands.

FIGURE 5-9 All controls are hidden while playing a video. Any tap reveals them, making discovery inevitable.

Strategically Unintuitive

The Seven Good Reasons for Unintuitive UI   **113**

- **Delighters**   Some apps reward expert users for their expertise, and expert users take pride in knowing things that ordinary users don't. **Well-designed delighters enhance the experience for experts without harming the experience for everyone else.**

    FIGURE 5-10   Delighters reward expert users for their expertise. Long press on the iPhone camera app reveals exposure controls.

- **Advanced modes**   As mentioned previously, you don't want users to find these modes accidentally or too easily.

    FIGURE 5-11   Long press reveals extended keys on a mobile keyboard. Advanced because most users don't need them.

- **Security and privacy**   Security and privacy concerns trump making interactions intuitive. The desire for intuitive interactions should never result in information disclosure, for example.

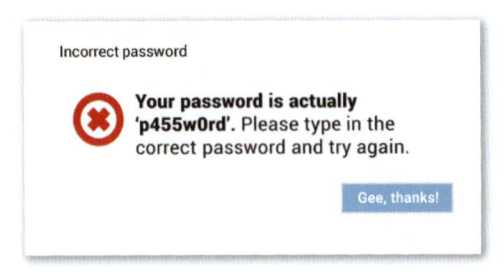

    FIGURE 5-12   Intuitive, but hardly secure.

114   Chapter 5   Strategically unintuitive

- **Significant destructive, irreversible actions** Irreversible and destructive actions with significant consequences should require thought—and lots of it. They shouldn't be efficient; users should have to go way out of their way to perform them.

FIGURE 5-13 Factory resets shouldn't be easy to do accidentally. iOS requires your password plus two confirmations.

Shortcuts and gestures

Let's explore the intuitiveness of shortcuts and gestures a bit more. A *shortcut* is an advanced interaction, usually requiring memorization, that lets a user perform a task more efficiently, whereas a *gesture* is a direct touch-based interaction with an object or content.

Given these definitions, the nature of shortcuts and gestures is to not have discoverability or affordance. If they did, they wouldn't be shortcuts or gestures; they'd be normal commands. Shortcuts and gestures require experimentation and memorization, so they aren't intuitive by definition. I consider the only intuitive gestures to be tapping an object with a tap affordance (such as a button or link), and possibly swiping an object with a slide affordance (such as a slider). And again, they aren't really gestures but normal commands.

Lacking intuitiveness isn't a problem for shortcuts and gestures as long as they are redundant. Keyboard shortcuts should always be redundant (Ctrl+Alt+Del for PCs is a notorious exception). Non-discoverable gestures are fine if there are equivalent fully intuitive interactions.

FIGURE 5-14 While the swipe-to-delete gesture isn't discoverable, but a redundant Trashcan icon would be.

Shortcuts and gestures   115

FIGURE 5-15 Long press is a shortcut for pasting copied text, like a phone number. While the Phone app gives no clue that this is possible, a user who copied a phone number is likely to try. Although not ideal, this is acceptable because of the intuitive alternative of entering the phone number manually.

Shortcuts and gestures are usually not discoverable and lack affordance, but this doesn't have to be the case. Keyboard shortcuts are often discoverable in desktop software, for example, through their documentation in menus and tooltips.

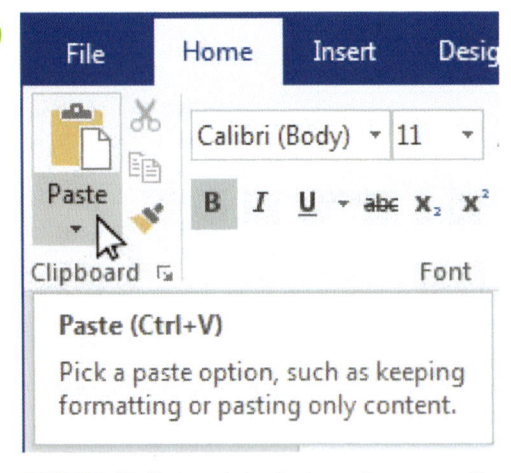

FIGURE 5-16 Keyboard shortcuts can have some discoverability through tooltips and menus.

116 Chapter 5   Strategically unintuitive

Even gestures can have discoverability through affordances.

If providing discoverability and affordance would be visually overwhelming statically, consider doing so dynamically.

FIGURE 5-17 How many gestures does the iOS Start screen support? How many of them are intuitive?

FIGURE 5-18 The swipe interaction is explained dynamically for five seconds. That works!

Intuitive

Although shortcuts and gestures are generally a good thing and will make expert users happy, don't overdo them. Both can be frustrating and annoying if users trigger them accidentally. If users perform disorienting gestures accidentally, they will definitely not be impressed by the intuitiveness of your app.

Tweet This!

Shortcuts and gestures   117

FIGURE 5-19 Backspace is a shortcut for Back? I don't think so! I'm glad this isn't enabled by default.

FIGURE 5-20 If you have a Mac with multiple side-by-side monitors, try dragging down at the bottom of the screen. Surprise! Ever done that accidentally (without knowing how)?

118   Chapter 5   Strategically unintuitive

Games and puzzles are different

Before continuing, I should mention that games and puzzles are different. We enjoy games and puzzles because they are challenging—they require thought and experimentation to figure out. They are deliberately missing the Eight Attributes of Intuitive UI because being too obvious would make the game no fun to play.

For example, the entire point behind the Where's Waldo? game is that Waldo isn't easily discoverable. What would a discoverable version look like? How about this?:

FIGURE 5-21 An intuitive Where's Waldo? No fun at all!

Unless our product is a game (or the successful result of gamification), having such challenges would be counterproductive. Nobody ever comes home from a hard day of work and thinks, "I just want to sit back and relax and try to figure out how Photoshop works."

The Levels of Intuitiveness chart

It's important to understand that an interaction that isn't fully intuitive—because it lacks some intuitive attributes—can still be quite usable. Or it can be a usability disaster, perhaps because it lacks all of them.

To help draw this distinction and give it some structure, I created the Levels of Intuitiveness chart:

FULLY INTUITIVE	These interactions are immediately self-explanatory because they have all the appropriate intuitive attributes. Users can achieve their desired outcomes without experimentation, memorization, documentation, or training.
SENSIBLE	These interactions often lack *discoverability* and *affordance*, but users figure them out through deduction and experimentation. Users remember them immediately—often on the first try—because they are based on real-world or standard interactions and are used consistently. Once learned, these interactions become routine and are described as intuitive by users because they require only trivial thought or experimentation.
LEARNABLE	Typically, these interactions are optional or more advanced and require learning because they are missing multiple intuitive attributes—often *discoverability* and *affordance*. They are used consistently, so most users learn them quickly, often by watching somebody else perform them. Once learned, these interactions are likely to be described as intuitive by users because they were learned so easily.
GUESSABLE	Typically, these interactions are optional or advanced and require experience to find and use because they are nonstandard and missing multiple intuitive attributes—often *discoverability*, *affordance*, *feedback*, or *predictability*. Not as consistent or expected as sensible and learnable interactions, these interactions are eventually learned and users can accurately guess where they might be used.
TRAINABLE	These interactions require documentation and training for users to perform successfully the first few times because they are nonstandard, poorly presented, or error-prone. With experience, users learn to perform them successfully without help or documentation.
BEYOND HOPE	These interactions so poorly designed that even documentation and training can't redeem them. Users can't perform these interactions successfully on their own—even experts struggle—because they are misleading or contradictory, lack feedback, or are error-prone. Users must rely on technical support, expert assistance, or training videos to get things done.

FIGURE 5-22 The Levels of Intuitiveness.

Let's work through this chart, using mobile gestures for examples. At the top, of course, is **fully intuitive**, which means that the UI has all the necessary Eight Attributes of Intuitive UI. At the bottom is poorly designed UI that even training or documentation can't save. It's the experiences in the middle—not fully intuitive but still usable—that are interesting.

Note that there is not one level but four. For mobile gestures, the only fully intuitive gesture is tap—all users know to tap UI elements that look interactive.

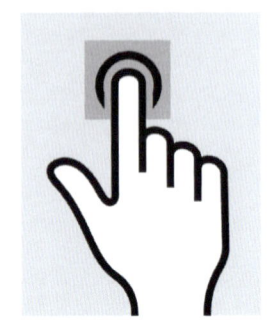

FIGURE 5-23 Tap is fully intuitive.

The top level of usable but not fully intuitive is **sensible**, which might lack discoverability or affordance, but **a sensible interaction is so natural that users will quickly experiment and discover that it works as expected.** (Here, *natural* can be defined as similar to real-world behaviors or well-known standard interactions or conventions.) Users would describe such interactions

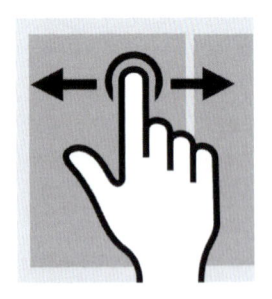

FIGURE 5-24 Swipe to navigate between documents is sensible.

Chapter 5   Strategically unintuitive

as intuitive, even though they don't strictly meet our definition because they require only trivial thought and experimentation. A good example here is *horizontal swipe* to navigate from one photo to another.

The next level is ***learnable***, which might also be missing discoverability or affordance and which isn't nearly as obvious as sensible. **I'm calling this learnable because users often learn these interactions by observing others.** Users still might describe such interactions as intuitive, even though they don't meet the definition. Good examples are *spread* and *pinch* gestures to zoom in and out of an image, or perhaps the *power + some other button* sequence for screen grabs. These gestures are easy to learn—once you see someone else do them—but you might not figure them out on your own.

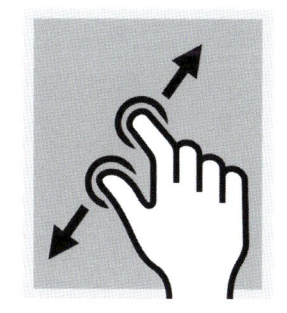

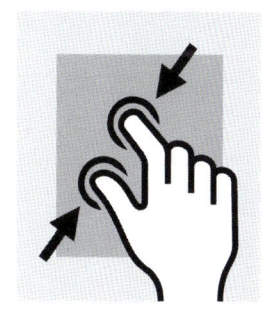

FIGURE 5-25 Spread and pinch to zoom in and out are learnable.

The next level is ***guessable***, which isn't nearly as obvious as sensible and might be missing multiple intuitive attributes. Frequent usage is often what makes these interactions usable. **Users learn these interactions through experience and are eventually able to guess accurately where to find them or how they work.** Good examples are the pull-down-to-refresh and pull-down-to-search gestures.

The last usable level is ***trainable*, which means that users must resort to training or documentation to use these interactions.** Often, they are nonstandard, poorly presented, or error-prone. As I made the case in Chapter 1, trainable is the level to avoid—unless you want to deliberately limit certain interactions to trained users. Consider sensible, learnable, or even guessable to be much better alternatives. A good example is the shake gesture for undo in iOS, which still few users know about.

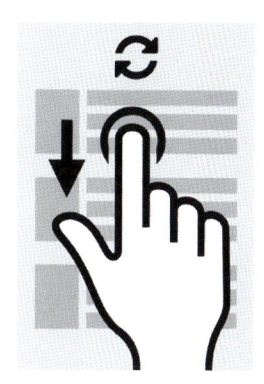

FIGURE 5-26 Pull-down-to-refresh and pull-down-to-search are guessable.

FIGURE 5-27 Shake is trainable.

So, why does all this matter? Because you lose more users as you work down the levels. For fully intuitive interactions, all users immediately get them, whereas for trainable interactions, *motivated* trained users *might* remember them, maybe.

The Levels of Intuitiveness chart **121**

Level	Description	
FULLY INTUITIVE	These interactions are immediately self-explanatory because they have all the appropriate intuitive attributes. Users can achieve their desired outcomes without experimentation, memorization, documentation, or training.	**All users will get**
SENSIBLE	These interactions often lack *discoverability* and *affordance*, but users figure them out through deduction and experimentation. Users remember them immediately—often on the first try —because they are based on real-world or standard interactions and are used consistently. Once learned, these interactions become routine and are described as intuitive by users because they require only trivial thought or experimentation.	
LEARNABLE	Typically, these interactions are optional or more advanced and require learning because they are missing multiple intuitive attributes—often *discoverability* and *affordance*. They are used consistently, so most users learn them quickly, often by watching somebody else perform them. Once learned, these interactions are likely to be described as intuitive by users because they were learned so easily.	
GUESSABLE	Typically, these interactions are optional or advanced and require experience to find and use because they are nonstandard and missing multiple intuitive attributes—often *discoverability, affordance, feedback*, or *predictability*. Not as consistent or expected as sensible and learnable interactions, these interactions are eventually learned and users can accurately guess where they might be used.	
TRAINABLE	These interactions require documentation and training for users to perform successfully the first few times because they are nonstandard, poorly presented, or error-prone. With experience, users learn to perform them successfully without help or documentation.	**Trained users *might* remember**
BEYOND HOPE	These interactions so poorly designed that even documentation and training can't redeem them. Users can't perform these interactions successfully on their own—even experts struggle—because they are misleading or contradictory, lack feedback, or are error-prone. Users must rely on technical support, expert assistance, or training videos to get things done.	

FIGURE 5-28 Why the intuitive levels matter.

Aim for fully intuitive or, if necessary, sensible and learnable. You lose more users as you work down the levels, so avoid trainable because in that case you are limiting the interaction to motivated trained users who have good memories.

Single-trial learning

People often ask me how single-trial learning fits into all this. *Single-trial learning* is the concept that some interactions are sufficiently self-explanatory that users learn them after a single trial.

Single-trial learning maps to the Levels of Intuitiveness perfectly. The key is to realize that there are two types of single-trial learning: when users attempt the trial on their own vs. when users learn by observing somebody and then performing a trial themselves. With that in mind, here is the mapping:

Sensible — Single trial, user figured out on own

Learnable — Single trial+, somebody showed user

Guessable — Multiple trials, user figured out on own

Trainable — Multiple trials, somebody showed user

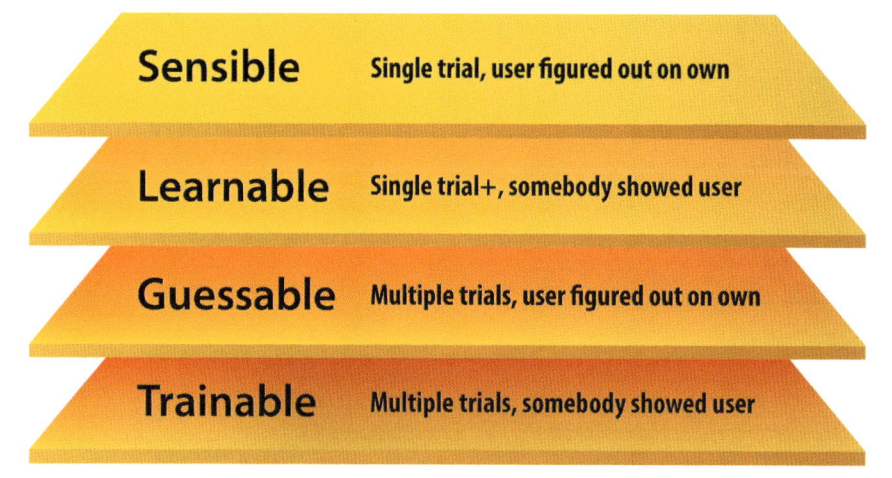

FIGURE 5-29 Mapping the Levels of Intuitiveness to single-trial learning.

***Sensible* and *learnable* are both forms of single-trial learning, but *guessable* and *trainable* often require multiple trials.** Research shows that users generally retain surprisingly little of what they learn, so an accurate name for the guessable and trainable levels might be *multiple-trial forgetting*. Skeptical? Here's a quick proof: Think of an app that you use frequently that has several cryptic custom icons. How many of those icons can you explain from memory? My bet: none! You have to relearn them each time.

FIGURE 5-30 Even though I use PowerPoint frequently, I still can't tell you what these icons mean without checking—and I have checked many times. And no, the first icon isn't edit and the third isn't search. (Answers: they are Pen/Highlighter and Zoom.)

Unintuitive

The definition of *intuitive UI*, revisited

Occasionally people argue with me about the definition of intuitive that I presented in Chapter 2. They will say something like, "I find the two-finger scroll totally intuitive, yet according to your definition it's not."

The definition of intuitive UI, revisited   **123**

My response is to stay focused on the main problem that we're trying to solve, which is that designers need a practical definition of intuitive UI. What is intuitive cannot remain an assertion of personal opinion. We need a simple, meaningful, objective definition that we can use to make practical assessments. **If we had a sufficiently broad definition to cover everything that anybody thought might be intuitive, such a definition would have no practical value.** So, if the two-finger scroll has no discoverability or affordance and there's no reason to try it or expect it but you immediately understand it once you see someone else use it, let's call that *learnable* instead of *intuitive*. You did have to learn it, after all, and making this distinction allows us to keep the definition of *intuitive* simple, meaningful, and objective.

Scoring tips

I'm often asked, "What if we score incorrectly? What if we decide an interaction is *sensible* when it's really *learnable*? After all, target users are different and their knowledge changes over time, so how do we know for sure?" To that, I have two answers.

The key is to score intuitiveness levels based on how users know or learn the interaction. If most target users can immediately figure it out on their own because it's based on real-world behaviors and conventions or well-known standards, it's *sensible*. If they quickly learn it from somebody else, it's *learnable*. If they learn it on their own through extensive experience and make mistakes along the way, it's *guessable*. And finally, if your users had to ask for help or resort to training, documentation, YouTube videos, etc., it's *trainable*. **Of course, this scoring should be based on the target users, not your personal opinion. Your knowledge of your app doesn't count!**

My second and preferred answer is that the exact score matters far less than the thinking and awareness behind it. Applying the Levels of Intuitiveness makes your team aware that not everything has to be intuitive, that making interactions intuitive requires tradeoffs, that there are different levels, and that the lower the level the more users you lose. There is no harm in assessing too low, but there is a penalty for assessing too high: unintentionally limiting your target market and harming user satisfaction.

Bottom line: if there is a simple, reasonable way to go up an intuitiveness level for important features and interactions, do it! Make them discoverable! Add the affordances! Make sure it's predictable!

Score the Levels of Intuitiveness based on how users know or learn. There's no benefit to inflating the score.

What about onboarding and coach marks?

It's common to see onboarding and coach marks being used to help users understand features and interactions, especially in mobile apps. *Onboarding* is a brief overview of an app that is displayed on first launch and that often explains how to use its (frankly) unintuitive features. By contrast, coach marks call out and explain the various features on a single page on demand.

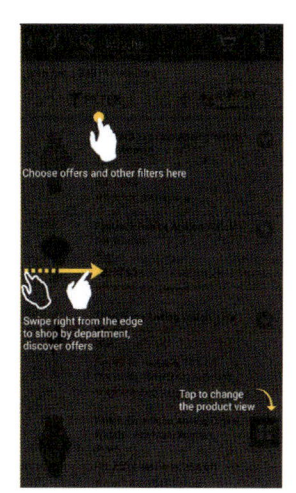

FIGURE 5-31 Examples of coach marks, which are common in mobile apps.

There are practical problems to these strategies: onboarding and coach marks make your app appear hard to use and unintuitive. Onboarding requires memorization and coach marks are a form of documentation, so by definition your app has announced it's not intuitive. They are also very easy to skip, which is by design, of course, but users often skip onboarding in particular because it appears at the wrong time. Users want to experience and explore your app first and learn the details later, when they're ready and motivated. To paraphrase Don Norman: *if your app's interaction needs coach marks, its design is probably faulty.*

Are onboarding and coach marks a good idea? They might be in special circumstances, but my assessment is usually not. The simplest way to decide is to ask, "Is there a practical alternative design that makes onboarding or coach marks unnecessary?" Almost always the answer is Yes. Nonstandard interactions are usually unnecessary and always risky.

Tweet This!

If your app has nonstandard gestures (that are hopefully redundant), the best approach is to display focused coach marks contextually, when the user is likely to use them and are motivated to learn them. If the gestures are especially useful, you can display them automatically in context—otherwise display them on demand.

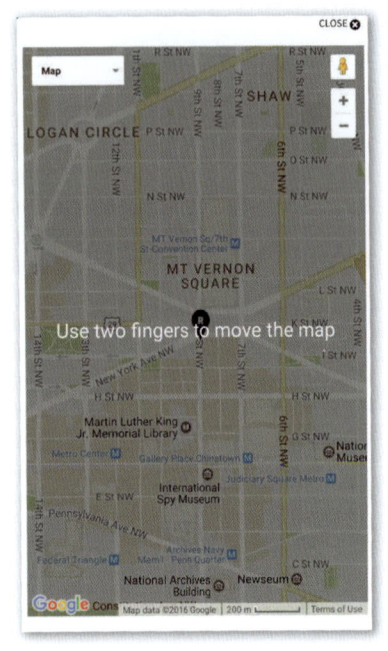

FIGURE 5-32 Display useful coach marks for nonstandard gestures contextually.

Let's look at an example. **For each coach mark, see if you can design a practical alternative that eliminates the need for the coaching.** Compare your results to mine at the end of the chapter.

126   Chapter 5   Strategically unintuitive

Example 1:

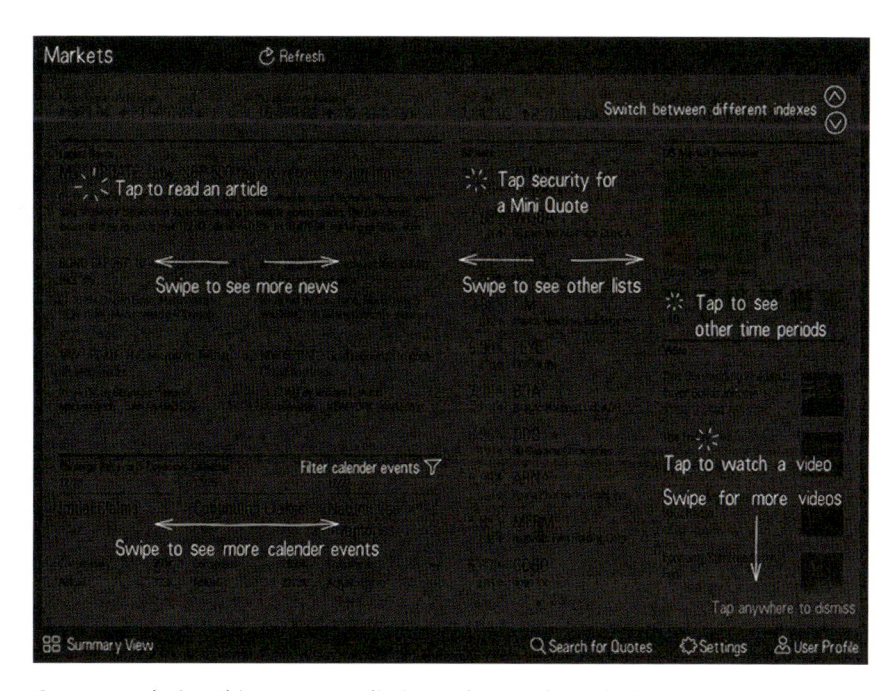

[Screenshot of a Markets screen with numerous coach marks overlaid, labeled "Unintuitive"]

Can you redesign this screen to eliminate the coach marks?

To help you get going, here are my guidelines for coach marks:

- To eliminate the need:
    - Use text labels, standard controls, and well-known icons and gestures when possible.
    - Use explicit commands in addition to gestures (example: The Trash command in addition to the *swipe-to-delete* gesture.)
    - Provide affordances to aid discoverability.
- For important nonstandard interactions:
    - Dynamically display individual coach marks in context. Stop displaying once the user successfully performs the interaction.
    - Enable users to learn by doing.
- When displaying coach marks:
    - If displayed automatically, do so contextually when relevant, at most three at a time (because the user didn't ask for the coaching so probably lacks motivation for more).

- If displayed on demand (via a Help button), you can show many more than three at a time because the user has expressed interest.

All this said, I am not completely opposed to onboarding. Like a modern user's manual (discussed in Chapter 1), effective onboarding should focus on demonstrating the app's value, not on explaining confusing, unintuitive UI. **Selling your app's value is crucial to its success, and effective onboarding can be perfect for that purpose.** Don't assume that users will immediately figure out your app's value themselves—or spend a lot of time doing so.

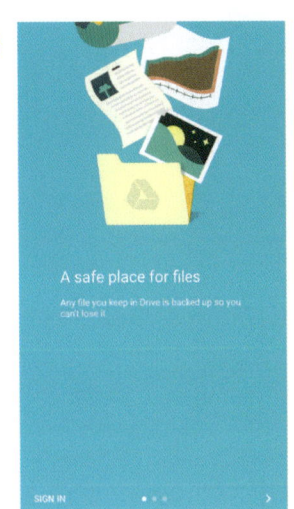

FIGURE 5-33 This onboarding is completely focused on demonstrating the app's value.

> Look for design alternatives that eliminate the need for onboarding and coach marks. Or use onboarding to demonstrate your app's value.

Strategically unintuitive

Let's now put everything in this chapter together into a single idea:

> *There is a cost to making a UI intuitive, and sometimes that cost isn't worth paying, so make sure you design unintuitive UI strategically rather than accidentally.*

All too often unintuitive UI is purely accidental.

Everett's Law of Intuitive UI

At this point, I will boldly proclaim *Everett's Law of Intuitive UI*, which I find to be true except for in the scenarios described in the Seven Good Reasons for Unintuitive UI:

> *For every unintuitive interaction, there is a possible preferable, intuitive interaction.*

Tweet This!

While I can't prove this law, I have found it very difficult to find good counterexamples. (If you find a good one, please send it to me at *everettm@intuitiveuibook.com* or post them on the Intuitive Design LinkedIn group.)

I recommend taking this law seriously. If you have an unintuitive UI that you can't justify strategically, try to find an intuitive alternative design. I bet you can. At the very least, you should be able to get to the next level in the Levels of Intuitiveness chart.

Summary

There's a cost to making a UI intuitive, and sometimes it's not worth paying the price or sometimes other considerations are more important. Shortcuts and gestures are common examples—they are great to have but not worth making intuitive. Using the Levels of Intuitiveness will help you make the right compromises. Remember that if an interaction can't be fully intuitive, making it sensible or learnable is a good alternative. Although a trainable UI can still be usable, requiring training will lose many users. But most importantly, make sure you design unintuitive interactions strategically rather than accidentally. All too often unintuitive interactions are purely accidental.

Exercises

Apply what you have learned in this chapter with the following exercises:

1. Find an example of a fully intuitive UI that would be better designed to be unintuitive. Which of the Seven Good Reasons for Unintuitive UI apply?

2. Find an example of an invisible shortcut or gesture that could be made discoverable. Evaluate the tradeoff. Is it worth making intuitive?

3. Find an example of a shortcut or gesture that doesn't have a fully intuitive equivalent. Is doing so justifiable? For example, is the command advanced, infrequent, or optional?

4. Find an example of a delighter. Explain why discovering it was really delightful. Did you miss the feature before you found it?

5. Find a good example of single-trial learning. Find a good example of multiple-trial forgetting. Why do you have a difficult time learning that interaction?

6. Find an example of onboarding or coach marks. Try to design an alternative that eliminates the need. Can you do it? Is it better?

7. Think of an app that you recently used that had onboarding. Recall and write down everything you remember, and then compare your notes to the onboarding screen. How much did you remember?

8. For a commonly used app, choose five interactions that are sensible and another five that are trainable. Do an informal survey of non-tech-savvy users and see who knows what. What percentage knew the sensible interaction? What percentage knew the trainable one?

9. Redesign a TV remote control to show only the most frequently used commands by default. How did you deal with the other commands? Is the result still intuitive? Is your solution better or worse than the original?

10. Is the QWERTY keyboard intuitive? If it is not fully intuitive, which intuitive level is it? Generally, what does your assessment tell you about keyboard-based interaction?

11. Is using Ctrl+Alt+Del to restart a computer intuitive? If not, is that a problem? Explain your answer either way.

12. If you are not already familiar, learn how to set up a HomeLink remote control in a car. Determine whether the process is intuitive by applying the definition of intuitive, the Eight Attributes of Intuitive UI, and the Levels of Intuitiveness. Design a new HomeLink setup process that is fully intuitive. What design elements are required to make this happen?

13. Review an app that you believe to be unintuitive by design (example: Snapchat). Characterize the interactions that are intuitive, as well as those that aren't. Try to rationalize the benefits of these unintuitive interactions—what were the designers trying to accomplish? How do you think these unintuitive interactions affect the success of the app, both short- and long-term?

My answers

EXAMPLE 1: We can eliminate the need for coach marks by using the following techniques:

- Tapping an article or video summary is a standard interaction, so coach marks aren't required. If we had data showing that users weren't understanding this, we could give these elements card affordances to subtly suggest interaction.

- Refresh, Search, and Settings are standard, well-known icons, so they don't need coach marks. Doubly true if they have text labels.

- User Profile and Filter are also standard icons, but they aren't well-known. We could eliminate the coach marks with text labels. We could access User Profile from Settings.

- Summary View is not a standard icon, but we could eliminate coach marks with a text label.

- Swipe-to-scroll is a standard interaction, but there are no scrollbars or other obvious scroll affordances. We could use arrow affordances or purposely render partial items to indicate scrolling.

Through more intuitive design, we could *easily* eliminate the need for the entire coach mark overlay.

CHAPTER 6

Intuitive task flows

Intuitive task flows answer the first question everybody has.

At this point, you know what it means for a UI to be intuitive, you understand the Eight Attributes of Intuitive UI, and you get that not everything needs to be intuitive. You're also familiar with the Levels of Intuitiveness, which help you make the right design tradeoffs.

You might now be thinking that there can't possibly be anything left to cover. Actually, there is—what you have learned so far is all you need to design an intuitive *individual* interaction, but what about a higher-level task flow in which multiple steps are required for a task to be successfully completed? For example, suppose that you're designing the checkout process for an e-commerce app. **Could you design all the individual interactions to be intuitive but still have an unintuitive task flow?**

The surprising answer is yes! In fact, this happens quite often. You need higher-level thinking to design intuitive, self-explanatory task flows—to eliminate the need for users to reason, experiment, memorize, or read documentation to get tasks done. In this chapter, you will learn simple techniques to achieve this goal.

Just as a user manual is a clear sign that a UI isn't intuitive, the need for an external task checklist is a clear sign that a task flow is unintuitive. The reason: A checklist is a summary of the important information needed by a user to perform a task that a UI simply fails to make obvious.

The task lifecycle

In Chapter 3, we used the interaction lifecycle to give structure to how users interact and then we looked for potential problems. Let's do the same for individual steps in a task:

1. The user navigates to the step, often by navigating to a new page. If the step is presented contextually, the user might need to scroll or do some other interaction to display the task pane.

FIGURE 6-1 Many task steps are contextual, such as searching and sorting.

2. The user scans the page or pane to figure out what to do. The first question all users have when they see a page for the first time is: *What am I supposed to do here?*

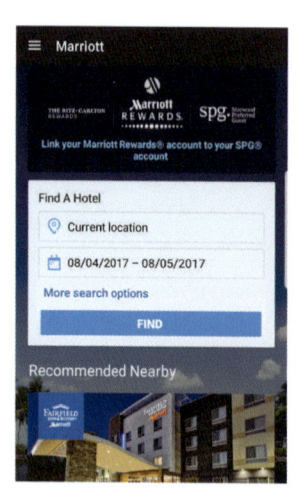

FIGURE 6-2 The first question all users ask: What am I supposed to do here? In this case, the labels clearly answer that question.

3. The user performs the step, often by providing input, making decisions, or performing substeps.

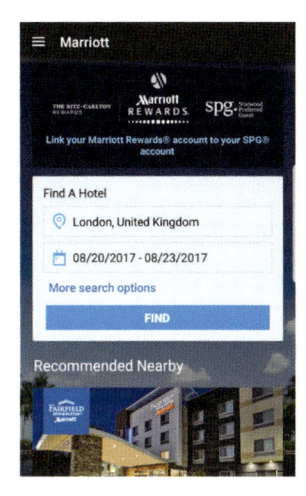

FIGURE 6-3 *Where* and *when* are decisions the user needs to make at this step.

4. The user reviews the actions and then commits to them. Committing either completes the task or advances the user to the next step required to complete the task (in which case this lifecycle repeats).

FIGURE 6-4 Tapping Book Now completes the task.

The task lifecycle   **135**

The trouble with task flows

What could go wrong during this task lifecycle? As in the case of the interaction lifecycle, plenty. Here are the potential problems for each step in a task flow:

1. The user can't find the step, navigates to the wrong one, or even skips the step. With the latter two cases, the user must recognize the mistake, recover (by navigating back), and find the right step.

2. The user can't figure out what to do or misunderstands what to do. In the latter case, the user must recognize the mistake and correct it, ideally before moving to the next step or completing the task incorrectly.

3. The user provides incorrect input or makes a poor choice. In this case, the user must recognize the mistake and correct it.

4. The user doesn't understand the commit model (instant vs. explicit commit), chooses the wrong commitment action, or doesn't realize that this step in the task is done.

Tweet This!

Task lifecycle steps 1, 3, and 4 are well addressed by the Eight Attributes of Intuitive UI described in Chapter 3. **What's new is step 2:** For intuitive task flows, the user must figure out what to do on the page quickly and correctly. Unfortunately, designers rarely put much effort into making each page's purpose obvious and self-explanatory. All too often a page is a collection of features whose purpose users have to figure out on their own.

> *For intuitive task flows, the user must figure out what to do on the page quickly and correctly. Usually designers put little effort into making the purpose of pages self-explanatory.*

Inductive UI

Tweet This!

I would like to introduce a concept, invented by Jan Miksovsky, that is known as *inductive UI*, which leads users through a set of self-explanatory task steps. Inductive UIs enable intuitive task flows, reducing the need for users to think and experiment to perform the steps. Such task flows easily lead or induce users through the steps. Crucially, inductive UIs answer that first question all users have when they see a page for the first time: What am I supposed to do here?

To explore this concept, let's start with the opposite of what we want, which we can call *deductive UI*. Do you see the problem with this dialog box?

What are you supposed to do on this page? The UI isn't saying, so you have to figure it out. Apparently, you need to tap the Add button—and hope that it's more obvious what to do next. **A better question: How did you figure that out? Most likely, you scanned the page, applied the process of elimination (a form of deductive logic), and deduced that the only productive action is tapping Add.** This design approach requires thought and experimentation, thereby turning task flows into little puzzles that users need to solve.

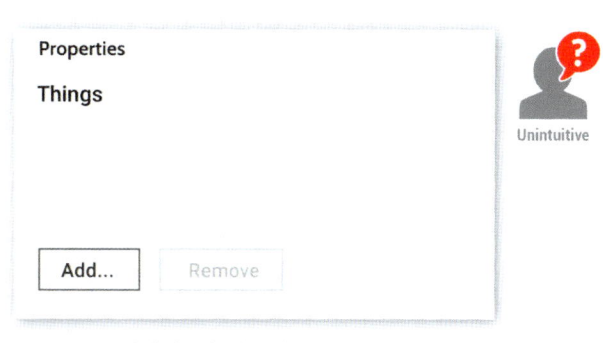

FIGURE 6-5 A deductive UI. What are you supposed to do here?

With the inductive approach, there's no question what to do because the page explicitly says so. Could users determine what to do on their own, without instructions? Probably…but why do we force users to figure this out—like some puzzle? Why don't we just tell them—at least when it doesn't go without saying?

If putting explicit instructions on a page strikes you as an odd idea, consider that we put titles on practically everything else to make them self-explanatory. Books have titles, chapter names, subheadings, figure captions, and so on. Imagine a book without chapter titles—users would have to read many pages just to figure out what a chapter is about. Too many task flows are like that.

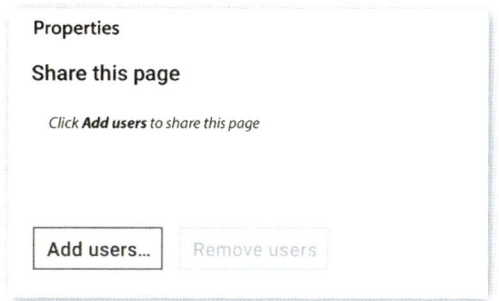

FIGURE 6-6 An inductive UI explicitly states what the user is supposed to do.

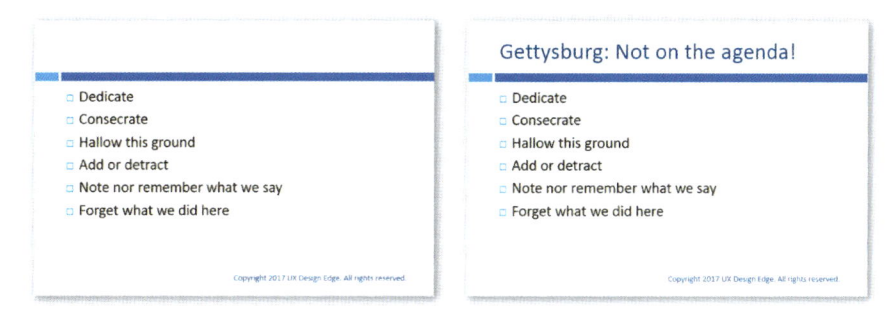

FIGURE 6-7 Which PowerPoint slide is easier to figure out? Which one looks more like your app's pages? Do you think it's a good idea to remove all the slide titles?

Inductive UI   **137**

Tweet This! **In Don't Make Me Think, Steve Krug boldly claims that "instructions must die." Do yourself a favor and ignore such advice.** Removing good instructions requires more thought from users! As a designer, you have ultimately three options when designing tasks:

- Option 1: Make all your screens self-explanatory without instructions.
- Option 2: Make all your screens self-explanatory *with* instructions.
- Option 3: Depend on experimentation, documentation, training, and tech support to get users through tasks.

A harsh reality check: Option 1 is very difficult to do, and all too often ends up being Option 3. Option 2 is the way to go.

Explainable first

The key to designing self-explanatory pages is to make them easily explainable—at the page level. That is, as the designer, you should be able to easily explain to somebody else what the purpose of the page is. **The concept: the easier it is for you as the designer to explain the purpose of the page, the easier it will be for your users to figure out that explanation on their own. I call this concept *explainable first*—because the goal of explainability drives the task design process.**

By contrast, if it is very difficult for you to explain the purpose of a page, it will be extremely difficult for users to figure out on their own. This is clear evidence that the page is poorly designed or perhaps even poorly understood by the design team. I often perform this exercise with my clients, and I've seen many examples where determining the purpose of a page required a 10-minute conversation. **Such pages are guaranteed to require training and documentation.**

FIGURE 6-8 Many tasks are like puzzles, where users must think and experiment to figure out what to do.

FIGURE 6-9 What is the purpose of this page? It's possible the designers don't know, because it lacks a clear purpose.

A task flow consisting of easily explainable pages is an easily understandable and intuitive task flow, so start task design by making each step explainable first.

Explainable first: The easier it is for you to explain the page's purpose to your users, the easier it will be for them to figure out its purpose on their own.

Designing main instructions

There is a simple tool that you can use to make pages explainable first: a main instruction. A *main* instruction is a heading that explains what users are supposed to do on a page. It is so called because it describes the entire page rather than a portion of the page, as ordinary instructions might. Here are some examples:

Designing main instructions   **139**

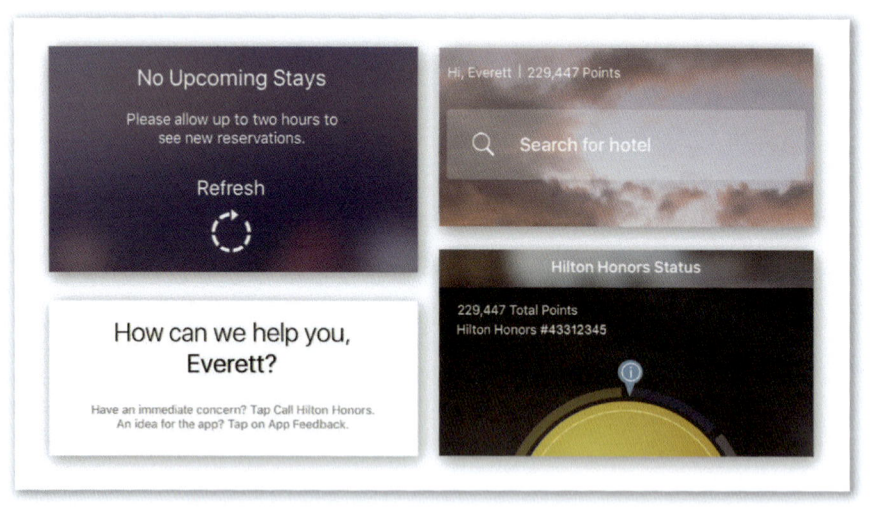

FIGURE 6-10 Some typical main instructions from a hotel app.

The process for using main instructions is simple: **When designing a task flow (before you design the individual pages for the task), start by designing a clear main instruction for each step in the task.** The benefit of this approach is that each page will have an easily explainable, well defined purpose—deliberately rather than accidentally. Doing so leads to better task flows and more intuitive pages.

But to be clear, you are *designing* these steps, not merely listing them. A well-designed set of main instructions takes some effort, but we can easily boil it down to a very simple concept: **Choose a main instruction that concisely matches what you would tell a target user in person *specifically* to do on the page. If it is concise, specific, and roughly matches what you would say, you have done it right.**

Let's work through an example of designing a main instruction for choosing photos to share:

- Attempt 1: **[no main instruction]**
  Most designers don't use main instructions, so this starting attempt is typical. But without an instruction, we haven't clearly defined what the page is for and we aren't telling the user either.

- Attempt 2: **Photos**
  This version feels mechanical. Yes, we have a page of photos, but what is the user supposed to do with them?

- Attempt 3: **Your photos**
  This version attempts to make the page more personal, but otherwise this has the same problem as attempt 2.

- Attempt 4: **Manage your photos**
  This version at least sounds like an actual instruction. But the word *manage* is vague. What exactly does manage your photos mean—pretty much anything, right? There is no clear, specific purpose. Importantly, you probably wouldn't tell the target user to *manage your photos*, right?

- Attempt 5: **Select your photo**
  This version is more specific, but based on the instruction it's not clear why the user needs to select a photo. And the user needs to select only one?

- Attempt 6: **Select your photos**
  This version realizes that the task might require multiple selection, but the reason for doing so still isn't stated.

- Attempt 7: **Select your photos to share with a friend**
  This version has almost everything we need—it's specific and roughly matches what we would say in person. Only problem: it's chatty. We want something more concise.

- Attempt 8: **Share your photos**
  This version has all the attributes of a good main instruction, plus it makes it very clear what the purpose of the page is—the user isn't selecting but sharing.

We took the "scenic route" to design this main instruction, but normally you can get to a good instruction more directly. **Think about what you would actually say to the target user, make sure it is useful and specific, and then get rid of any unnecessary words.** That's where you want to be.

Design task flows by designing the main instructions first and then using them to design the pages. Choose concise main instructions that match what you would say in person.

Tweet This!

Designing page integrity

Per the process, we came up with these previous main instructions without having an existing page design. This is crucial. **We aren't just labeling an existing page design—*we are using the main instruction to determine the page design*. Both designing the main instruction and using it to design the page itself are crucial for making intuitive task flows.**

To see how this works, let's evaluate the impact the main instruction has on the page design. A page labeled "Manage your photos" might look like this:

Designing page integrity   **141**

FIGURE 6-11 A photo gallery page designed to "manage" photos, whatever that means.

By contrast, a page labeled "Share your photos" might look like this:

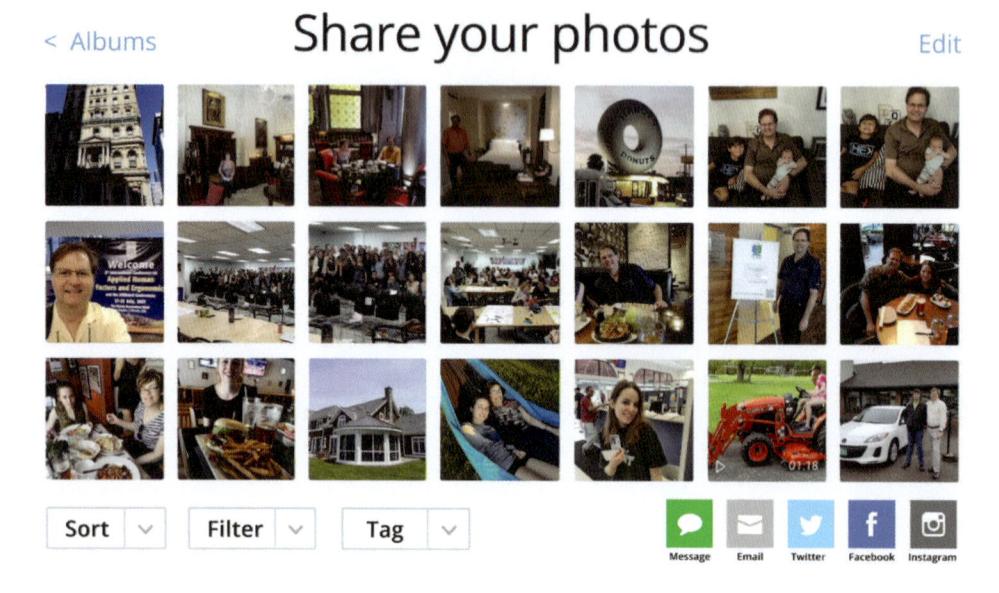

FIGURE 6-12 A page designed specifically for sharing photos.

142   Chapter 6   Intuitive task flows

A well-designed main instruction acts as a framework to help you determine what belongs on the page and what is most important. Using main instructions leads to page designs that have *integrity and focus*. By contrast, a page designed with a vague instruction—again, the verb *manage* often results in vagueness—or no instruction at all is likely to just be an organized pile of features or design patterns. Dashboards often have this problem—they are designed without any particular purpose and are just a pile of dashboardy stuff.

For example, suppose a page is labeled "Select Photos." For that specific purpose, I would expect a well-designed page to have these selection features:

- Sort by name, date, location, rating, tags, and file size.
- Filter by tags, date ranges, and ratings.
- Filter out poor focus, poor exposure, and duplicates.
- Mark favorites.
- Automatic grouping of related photos (same subject taken at same time).

Such a page would be designed expressly for narrowing down a large collection of photos to a subset of desired photos with speed and ease. By contrast, most of these selection capabilities would be missing from a more general "Manage Your Photos" page.

To summarize the process: use main instructions when designing task flows to 1) make each page of the task flow self-explanatory, 2) make sure the pages have integrity and focus, and 3) get the mechanics and details right. Unfortunately, many designers start with the third goal and completely skip the first two.

We'll look at several examples in a moment, and you'll see the power of main instructions. **You'll see that the quality of the main instruction predicts the quality of the page.** The better the main instruction, the better the resulting task step. Also, if a task flow is complex, convoluted, unnatural, or unintuitive, it should be apparent just by reviewing the instructions themselves. The series of main instructions can make it obvious that your task flow itself needs to be improved.

You might be thinking, *But I already do all that when I'm designing pages.* Perhaps you do, but I've observed many designers who don't. **When designing individual pages, we usually get too bogged down with the details too early. We're so focused on features, layout, flow, controls, and details (such as icons and colors) that we fail to design the page as a whole.**

> *For page integrity, make sure everything on the page is clearly related to its main instruction.*

Designing page integrity

Working through two examples

We've just reviewed a process for designing new task flows—start by designing the main instructions and design the actual pages later—but **here's a variation for redesigning an existing page:**

1. Determine what a good main instruction for the page would be (and make it *specific, concise, and matching what you would say in person*). Choose this main instruction based on what the step should be, which might be quite different from the existing page design.

2. Evaluate the existing page's design based on that instruction (*Is the design self-explanatory? Does the content match the instruction?*)

3. If not, redesign both to match each other.

4. If the main instruction doesn't go without saying—that is, if the page's purpose still isn't self-explanatory—actually put the main instruction on the page.

Having a clear understanding of what a page is for makes it better—even if you don't display the main instruction on the page! Let's redesign two real UIs using this process.

Design Challenge 1: A tool for web developers

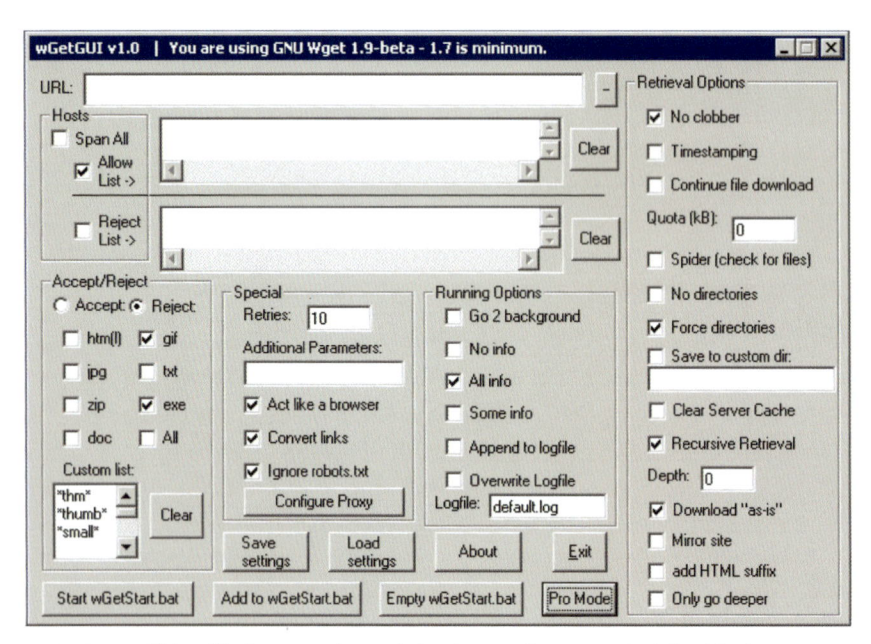

FIGURE 6-13 This utility is targeted at web developers. Can you make it intuitive?

Design Challenge 2: Configuring a virtual machine

FIGURE 6-14 This page allows users to choose the hardware configuration for a virtual server. Can you make it intuitive?

The key to both of these design challenges, which should be very clear at this point, is to start by designing a good main instruction. The rest of the page design follows naturally. **Compare your designs to mine at the end of the chapter.**

I have used this design approach for years, and I continue to be impressed by how well it works. This quote from Albert Einstein concisely states what this technique is all about.

> *If I had an hour to solve a problem and my life depended on it, I would use the first 55 minutes determining the proper question to ask, for once I knew the proper question, I could solve the problem in less than five minutes.* –Albert Einstein

That "proper question" for intuitive page design is the main instruction.

When to *not* display a main instruction

At this point, I hope it's clear that the inductive UI concept—using main instructions to design self-explanatory pages—has tremendous value. **The concept isn't about having chatty pages with silly instructions that clearly aren't necessary. Rather, it's about designing intuitive task flows and pages with integrity. It's about eliminating the need for training and documentation at the task level.** That's a huge benefit from such a simple technique.

Still, as a UX design trainer who instructs dozens of workshops per year, I have noticed that although some designers eagerly embrace the concept, **many designers are terrified to put instructions on their pages, even when the need is obvious.**

How do you tell when the need is obvious? Easy: during a design presentation or design review, the first thing the designer explains is the missing main instruction for a page. If that instruction is important enough to explain explicitly when the designer is in the room, it's clearly important enough to state explicitly when the designer isn't there so that users understand how to use the page.

Unintuitive

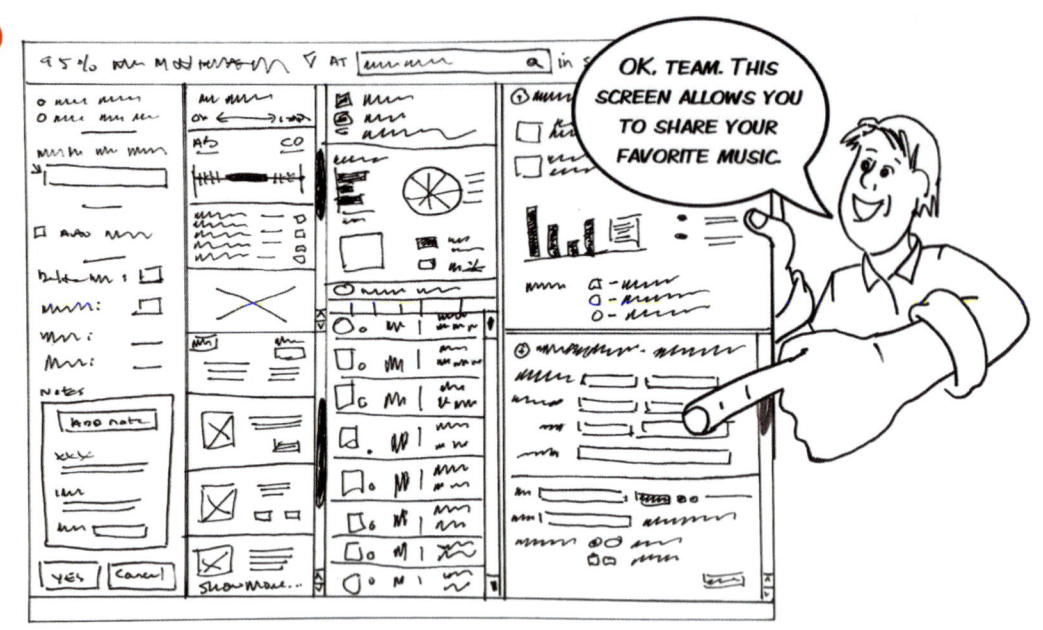

FIGURE 6-15 The designer's explanation clearly shows that this page needs a main instruction.

Another situation when the need is obvious: when users must scroll the page to figure out what to do. Modern responsive design often results in extensive scrolling (who decided that's a good idea?), so this is especially a concern with responsive design. **Reports of the demise of designing "above the fold" (that is, content users can see without scrolling) are greatly exaggerated. Users should never have to scroll to determine if they are on the right page or the purpose of the page.** See the next section for more on this problem.

Tweet This!

146   Chapter 6   Intuitive task flows

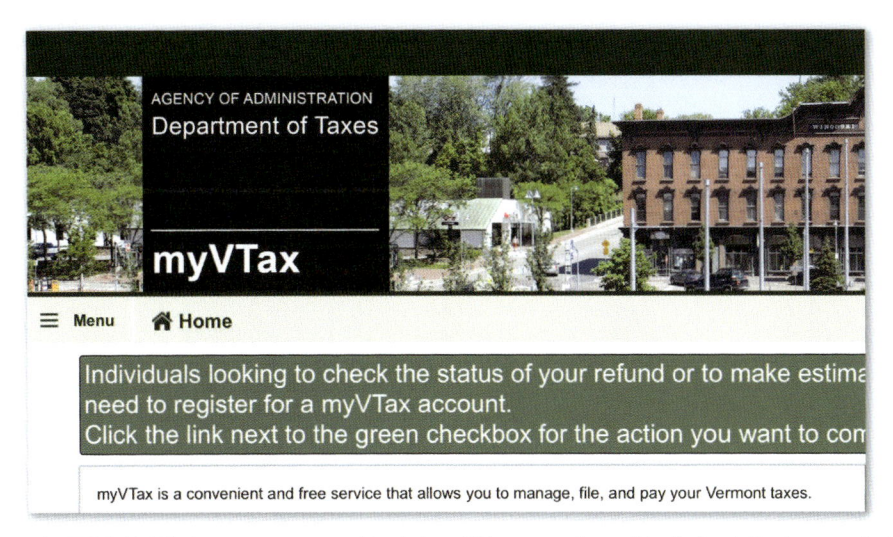

FIGURE 6-16 What are you supposed to do here? Users must scroll to find out. Having a main instruction removes all doubt.

That said, there are situations where an explicit main instruction isn't needed. We can still apply the inductive UI design process to get the other benefits; we just leave out the instruction from the final design.

Here are common situations where the main instruction doesn't need to be explicitly on the page:

- For easy-to-recognize, standard pages.
- When it is a trivial restatement of the page content or even the purpose of the app.
- When the result just feels chatty and unhelpful.

FIGURE 6-17 In this case, you can skip the main instruction.

When to not display a main instruction   147

If it's a close call and you can't decide, err on the side of being intuitive and give the main instruction. For a close call, some users might find the instruction obvious, but they will skip right over it without even noticing. Users who benefit from the instruction will appreciate the extra clarity and confidence. Users won't wonder if they are in the right place (which, as you recall, is a potential problem for the first step of the task lifecycle).

Don't display the main instruction if it clearly goes without saying. But if you aren't sure, err on the side of being intuitive by including the instruction.

FIGURE 6-18 Users can figure out that they are supposed to make a payment here, but the main instruction adds clarity and instills confidence.

What about responsive design?

Most modern websites are using *responsive design*, which uses flexible layouts, images, and styles to adapt to any screen size and orientation. Responsive design often results in tasks that require scrolling through very long pages instead of navigating to shorter ones. **Doesn't responsive design change everything? Surprisingly, not really. Let's take a look at why that's true.**

Responsive designs often have a significantly different task flow model, where users interact using the following steps:

1. Review the large, mostly useless hero image (a large, prominent banner image) above the fold to recognize visually that this is a responsive design.

2. Do not find what they are looking for, so start scrolling.

3. Scroll, scroll, scroll.

4. Scroll, scroll, scroll.

5. Find the large, mostly useless fat footer to visually recognize that they have finally reached the end of the interminably long page.

6. Desperately hope that perhaps what they are looking for is hidden in the hamburger menu.

7. Try a command in the hamburger menu. (Nope, not there either—commands there just scroll to a section on the page.)

I'm exaggerating a bit, but this is the unfortunate (and unnecessary) state-of-the-art responsive design style at the time of this writing. Misuse of the responsive design clichés often results in what I call Terrible UX from Responsive Designs (or *TURDs*).

Responsive task flows are often not broken into pages but into sections instead. I believe the need for good instructions is actually even stronger for these responsive page sections than for more traditional page-based design. Here's why:

- **Having instructions—you might call these *section instructions*—helps users scan the page sections.** Users shouldn't have to read the sections carefully to figure out what they are for. Remember the first question that all users have: *What am I supposed to do here?*

- **Navigating to a page provides context and indicates intent, whereas scrolling alone gives no context.** In traditional page-based navigation, the user has to perform an explicit action to navigate to the next page, and this action provides context. For example, by tapping Checkout, the user is explicitly stating interest in completing a purchase. By contrast, scrolling down on a long responsive page does not provide any specific context or reflect any specific intent.

To put everything together, let's see how a particularly good use of section instructions makes the content of a responsive page much easier to scan and comprehend. These section instructions tell the whole story, and I believe they are the most important content on the page. Today, many responsive pages skip them.

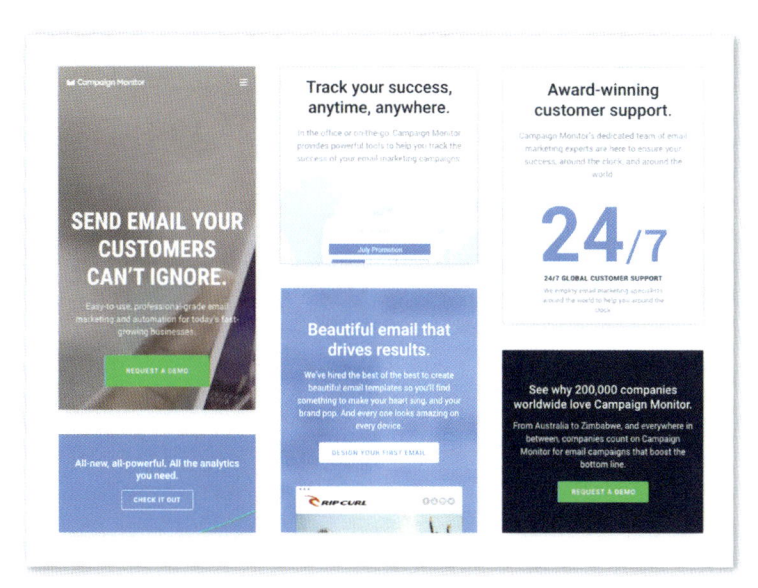

FIGURE 6-19 Campaign Monitor uses section instructions to tell a clear, compelling story on a responsive page. I know what's on the page by reading the section instructions alone. By contrast, many responsive pages without section instructions essentially say *Here's a bunch of stuff. Scroll through it and figure it out yourself.*

Long responsive pages need an instruction for each section.

What about responsive design?   **149**

Summary

The first question all users have when they see a page for the first time is: *What am I supposed to do here?* Surprisingly, we rarely answer this question in our designs, but doing so is required for intuitive task flows. Intuitive task flows are easily explainable, so start your page design by focusing on explainability. Having main instructions not only makes pages self-explanatory (reducing the need for documentation and training), but also helps ensure that those pages' designs have integrity and focus. Best of all, *explainable first* makes your overall design process more efficient by helping you find task flow problems sooner.

Designers are often afraid to put main instructions on their pages. If the purpose of the page isn't obvious, give the instruction explicitly. (When in doubt, just do it!)

Exercises

Apply what you have learned in this chapter with the following exercises:

1. Find an example of a confusing task flow, where the interaction on the pages is intuitive but the overall task across those pages isn't. Why is it confusing? Do you have to think or experiment to figure out the pages? Propose an alternative design to improve the task flow.

2. Find a nontrivial task flow that doesn't use main instructions and add them. Evaluate the task flow now. Is it improved?

3. Find an example of a task flow that has ineffective main instructions. Why are they ineffective? Rewrite them or justify removing them.

4. Find three examples of task steps for which having an explicit main instruction would be unnecessary. Justify your assessment. Do these unnecessary main instructions (or their pages) have anything in common?

5. Design a generic view page to view a list of results of some task. Now consider specific types of view pages, such as Confirm (a reservation), Purchase (from a shopping cart), and Enroll (a college class schedule). Design a main instruction for each variation and determine appropriate changes for each so that the page design better matches the more specific instruction.

Answers

Design Challenge 1: A tool for web developers

For this makeover, I had to spend about 10 minutes reviewing the utility's user manual to figure out what the program does. It's not obvious. **The main instruction I came up with is *Copy website files for backup and offline viewing*. Once I had that, the redesign was easy because copying files is a familiar design pattern.**

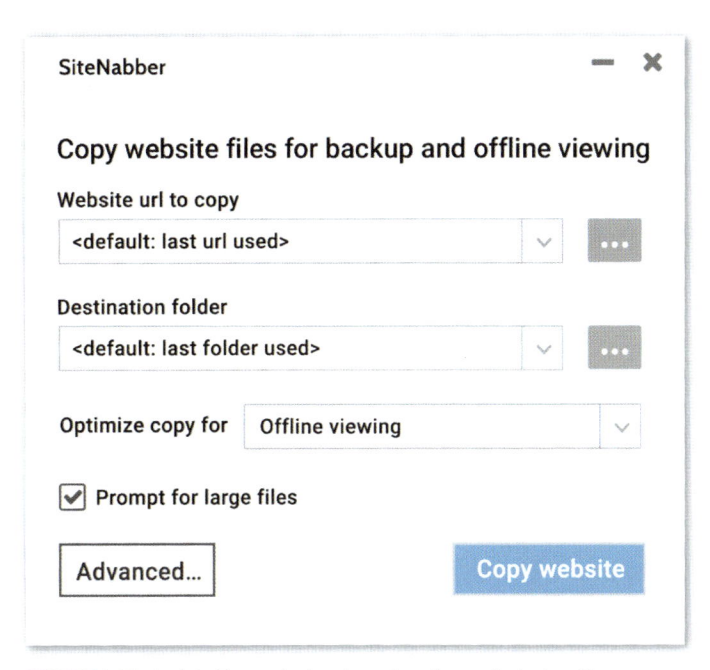

FIGURE 6-20 An intuitive redesign based on the main instruction.

Because the main instruction isn't obvious, I put it directly on the screen. The only challenge is deciding which options are important enough or get changed frequently enough to justify surfacing them directly on the main window. This decision requires some user research.

Design Challenge 2: Configuring a virtual machine

For this makeover, the main instruction might not be obvious if you have never used such a tool, but **the main instruction I came up with is *Choose the most cost-effective server configuration that supports your application.***

FIGURE 6-21 An intuitive redesign based on the main instruction.

Given this main instruction, the now-obvious problem with the original design is that there is no indication of what minimum hardware configuration is needed to support the application, nor any indication of cost. Without this critical information, how does the user make an informed decision? The redesign recommends server configurations based on the application requirements (selected in Step 2), plus sorts them according to their monthly cost. Because this main instruction is a restatement of what is now clearly on the page, there is no reason to display it explicitly.

CHAPTER 7

A design process for intuitive UI

The proof of an intuitive pudding is target users doing intuitive eating.

This chapter focuses on adapting your team's design process so as to more effectively design intuitive UIs. I'm not assuming that you're using any particular design process—my goal isn't to give an exact step-by-step process but rather to show you how to supplement what you're currently doing.

Maximizing the value of usability testing

It's crucial to have good tools to evaluate the intuitiveness of your designs. I recommend both usability testing as well as *expert* evaluations (also called *inspection methods*). While usability testing is the most dependable measure of success (because it evaluates real users performing real tasks), it can be relatively expensive and time consuming to perform—which is a problem in our increasingly agile world. Furthermore, a merely usable UI isn't that high of a bar. (Aaron Walter aptly compares *usable* design to *edible* food. You can and should do better.)

The key is that effective expert evaluations make usability testing much more productive. People often use a chart like this one to determine the number of participants for a usability study.

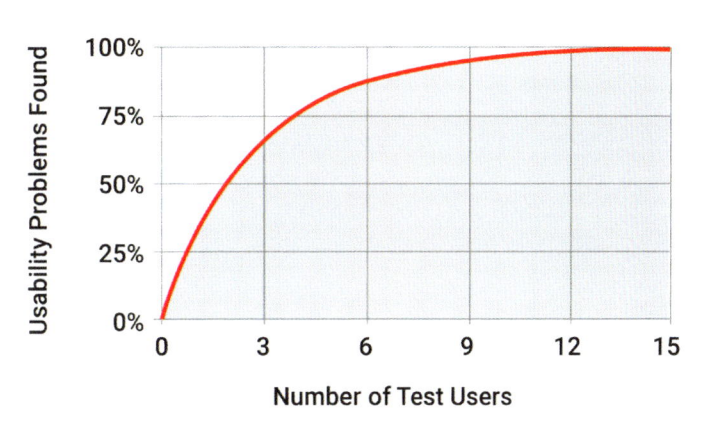

FIGURE 7-1 A chart that shows diminishing returns for additional test participants. Made famous by Jakob Nielsen but based on research by Robert Verzi.

Often, this chart is used to claim that six test participants is optimal. **But I am going to make the radical claim that the y-axis is often mislabeled. It should say** *Most obvious usability problems found.* **In practice, during a usability study we usually find the most obvious problems that remain.** Suppose, for example, we do a usability study that finds 20 problems and we design another iteration that fixes those problems without adding new ones. Almost certainly, the next round of usability testing will reveal perhaps 20 more usability problems that were obscured by the previous batch. **The bottom line: On its own, one round of usability testing isn't likely to be enough, regardless of the number of participants.**

Tweet This!

For your team to do its best work, it must be able to find routine design problems on its own, without being dependent on usability testing. **To be efficient, reserve usability testing for the design problems that you can't readily find.** This will reduce the number of rounds of usability testing required.

> While usability testing is the most dependable measure of success, you can make it more effective and efficient by preceding it with expert evaluation techniques to find routine design problems first.

A process for making intuitive design decisions

You've learned how to make intuitive design decisions throughout the book, so now let's put everything together in a simple process for designing an intuitive interaction—starting with a design proposal:

1. **Grade the intuitiveness of the proposed interaction.**
   The grades are *fully intuitive, sensible, learnable, guessable, trainable,* and *unusable,* as defined in Chapter 5 and summarized in the Glossary. If you aren't sure, consider usability testing of a prototype right away to grade the design.

2. **Determine whether the interaction is important.**
   Consider the interaction important if it's needed by most users for routine tasks. Consider it unimportant if it is advanced, infrequent, or optional. If you aren't sure, consider user research to determine importance.

   a. **If the interaction is important, aim for *fully intuitive*. If already there, done!**

   b. **If the interaction is unimportant and *fully intuitive* isn't practical, aim for *sensible*, *learnable*, or *guessable*. If already there, done!**

3. **Improve the design to match the target grade. If successful, done!**
   Determine where the Eight Attributes of Intuitive UI are weakest, and focus there.

4. **Otherwise, try alternative designs. If the design is only *trainable* or *unusable*, keep going.**

To summarize this process in less-flowcharty language:

Use the importance of the interaction plus the Levels of Intuitiveness (from Chapter 5) to see if there is a problem. Use the Eight Attributes of Intuitive UI (Chapter 3) both to help determine the Level of Intuitiveness and to identify what specifically needs improvement. Not everything has to be fully intuitive, but you should avoid designs that require training and documentation. Consider completely different designs if the design being evaluated can't be improved sufficiently.

In practice, I find this process easy to apply for routine design problems and still quite helpful for more complex ones. The key to success is to not get too hung up on the details. Exact answers aren't required—close answers are usually good enough.

Let's try it with a real example:

> *Suppose your team is designing a new version of a popular operating system. The proposed design hides the entry point for all program interactions, such as program launching, and reveals it with a hidden, nonstandard interaction. Is this design proposal acceptable?*

Good question! You might already know the answer, but let's apply the intuitive design decision-making process I described above to find out:

1. **Grade the intuitiveness of the proposed interaction.**
   The grade for this interaction is *learnable* at best or *trainable* at worst. Why? The first attribute of intuitive UI is discoverability, which this proposal clearly lacks—the interaction isn't easily discoverable by design. (Notice that I'm using the Eight Attributes of Intuitive UI to help me determine the level of intuitiveness.) A grade of *sensible* is impossible because the interaction is nonstandard and therefore not obvious to the target users.

2. **Determine whether the interaction is important.**
   This interaction is very important because it is used by all users for routine tasks.

   a. **If the interaction is important, aim for *fully intuitive*. If already there, done!**
      Definitely not there yet!

   b. **If the interaction unimportant and if *fully intuitive* isn't practical, aim for *sensible*, *learnable*, or *guessable*. If already there, done!**
      N/A because the interaction is important, so skip.

3. **Improve the design to the target grade. If successful, done!**
   Can easily fix by having (or in this case, maintaining) an easily discoverable program access point on the screen. Done!

4. **Otherwise, try alternative designs. If the design is only *trainable* or *unusable*, keep going.** N/A, so skip.

The best part of this design process is that it is driven by objective criteria instead of personal opinion. Once you get the hang of it, applying this process to a design problem should take about a minute. Seriously! That's how long it should take to realize it's unacceptable for an important feature to have poor discoverability. And doing so quickly leads to good solutions. Of course, we still need to test our resulting design, but we won't waste our time discovering problems that should have been obvious when viewed from the proper (is it intuitive?) perspective.

Grading intuitiveness

As you've seen, the first step of the process for making intuitive design decisions is grading the intuitiveness of the proposed interaction. How do you do that exactly? **You assess the interaction for the Eight Attributes of Intuitive UI, using a simple Pass/Fail for each attribute. Is it plausible that the target users would agree that the attribute is present? If so, that's a Pass. If an attribute is missing, ask whether it's plausible that the target users would agree that the attribute's absence isn't a problem. If that answer is yes, that's also a Pass. If not, it's a Fail.** This simple grading scheme works because problems are usually obvious and flagrant, such as a critical intuitive attribute outright missing for a frequently used interaction. You don't have to think too hard with these.

For the Levels of Intuitiveness, I use the following grading:

- **Sensible**   Does the interaction follow well-known standards, apply real-world conventions, or match knowledge from the target user's prior experience? If so, it's *sensible* because there's a realistic chance that users will quickly figure it out through a little thought or experimentation.

- **Learnable**   Is it like *sensible*, but most likely users quickly learned it from somebody else instead of on their own? If so, that's *learnable* by definition.

- **Guessable**   Does the interaction follow a pattern that isn't well known to the target users or is inconsistently applied? Is there a realistic chance that users will figure it out on their own with sufficient experience? If so, that's *guessable*.

- **Trainable**   Did you have to ask for help, check documentation, or search the web? If so, it's *trainable*.

I find this grading is fairly easy to apply, but **it's important that you check your personal knowledge of how the UI works at the door.** Make these assessments based on what target users already know or see on the screen, not on your own experience with the app. The fact that you and your team know exactly how it works means nothing.

The Seven Levels of UX Persuasion

You've learned a variety of tools and techniques that you and your team can use to make sure your designs are intuitive. I'd like to add just a few more finishing touches here.

We've seen the importance of having a specific, shared vocabulary. As I mentioned in Chapter 4, if you were to say only that my proposed UI design is unintuitive, frankly I'd expect that conversation to lead nowhere. How can I fix the problem if I don't know what it is? By contrast, if you were to say that my design has an important feature with poor discoverability, a misleading affordance, and an incomprehensible label, I know exactly what that means and exactly what to do about it. Having a specific, shared vocabulary allows us to communicate and collaborate, rather than talk past each other.

FIGURE 7-2 Better vocabulary, better collaboration.

Different types of arguments, including those using a shared vocabulary, have different levels of persuasion. To give this some structure, I've created The Seven Levels of UX Persuasion:

7 Beauty, visual design, emotion, delight, brand
6 Scenarios, personas, user goals, value, satisfaction
5 Usability, real user data, conversion, other metrics
4 Design principles, guidelines, patterns, consistency
3 Mechanical usability, business goals
2 Technology, code, UI frameworks
1 Personal opinion, "gut" instinct, "Trust me I'm the designer"

More Persuasive ← → Less Persuasive

User Centered ← → Technology Centered

FIGURE 7-3 The Seven Levels of UX Persuasion.

Tweet This!

To work this through, note that everybody's favorite method of persuasion—their own personal opinion—is rock bottom at Level 1. Developers think in terms of the technology capabilities and constraints, which is Level 2 and usually trumps personal opinion. Managers, by contrast, are focused on business goals, Level 3, which usually trumps both designers and developers. **Using the Eight Attributes of Intuitive UI works well because it uses design principles (Level 4).** You might be surprised that user research data is Level 5, not Level 7. The way I see it, data metrics such as conversion (Level 5) without user satisfaction (Level 6) leads to designs that are dark patterns—essentially user manipulation.

To finish the levels, Level 6 addresses user-centered design: who the users are (personas), what they are trying to do and the context in which they are doing it (scenarios and goals), what value they get from your app, and ultimately their satisfaction with it. Level 7 works at the emotional level. No matter how rational you think your users are, people react emotionally, so factors like beauty, delight, and branding can be very persuasive—assuming the basic functionality is properly designed.

To prevail over routine technology and business concerns, you need to work at Level 4 or higher, and the tools and techniques described in this book enable you to work at Levels 4 and 5. If you can then tie the intuitive attributes to fulfilling your product's value proposition and its top user scenarios, that puts your work at Level 6. Hard to beat!

Chapter 7   A design process for intuitive UI

A real-world persuasion scenario

Let's work through a realistic situation that calls for some persuasion:

> *Suppose you are the lead designer for a newly released product and discover that a poorly designed UI has become a top tech support call generator. You file a bug to get it fixed, but your team's lead developer resolves the bug as "Won't fix—superficial cosmetic detail. Just explain it in the documentation."*

How do you get your engineering manager (who is under pressure to maintain the schedule and developer velocity) on board to overrule the dev lead? (By the way: This is not an entirely made-up example.)

Let's start with some techniques that won't work (which you might know from experience):

- Claiming that intuitive UI is personal and subjective, so the dev lead is wrong and you are right.
- Saying "Trust me, I'm a designer!"
- Claiming that intuitive UI is familiar or learnable, and you need to make the product more learnable with a redesign to reduce tech support costs.
- Claiming that intuitive UI is like a magic escalator of acquired knowledge, and you need to redesign the UI to move users up the escalator. (Long story behind this one...)

These are flimsy arguments that aren't likely to be persuasive.

Here's an approach that *will* work:

1. Determine the amount of money on the table—provide a real number of how much money is wasted on tech support because of poor design.
2. Determine the specific cause of the problem.
3. Propose a design that solves the specific problem.
4. Demonstrate that the proposed design is better, using the Eight Attributes of Intuitive UI vocabulary as needed.
5. (If time) Perform a usability study to verify the proposed design fixes the problem.

Working at a higher level of UX persuasion, having a tested (not hypothetical) solution, presenting it to your team with an objective design vocabulary, and showing that solving the problem leads to reducing costs with real numbers—this approach wins!

Traditional heuristic evaluations

A *heuristic evaluation* is a team-based expert evaluation, where "experts" (most likely, members of your team) evaluate a design based on compliance with established design heuristics. *Design heuristics*, in turn, are a set of recognized (by independent parties) usability principles. The goal of heuristic evaluation is to leverage existing knowledge to find "obvious" design problems quickly and, ideally, make usability testing more productive.

Many design heuristics exist, but the most famous set was published in Jakob Nielsen's *Usability Engineering* and were originally devised by Nielsen and Rolf Molich in 1990. Here's a summary:

- **Visibility of system status**   The system should always keep users informed about what is going on, through appropriate feedback within reasonable time.

- **Match between system and the real world**   The system should speak the user's language, with words, phrases and concepts familiar to the user, rather than system-oriented terms. Follow real-world conventions, making information appear in a natural and logical order.

- **User control and freedom**   Users often choose system functions by mistake and will need a clearly marked "emergency exit" to leave the unwanted state without having to go through an extended dialogue. Support undo and redo.

- **Consistency and standards**   Users should not have to wonder whether different words, situations, or actions mean the same thing. Follow platform conventions.

- **Error prevention**   Even better than good error messages is a careful design that prevents a problem from occurring in the first place. Either eliminate error-prone conditions or check for them and present users with a confirmation option before they commit to the action.

- **Recognition rather than recall**   Minimize the user's memory load by making objects, actions, and options visible. The user shouldn't have to remember information from one part of the dialogue to another. Instructions for use of the system should be visible or easily retrievable whenever appropriate.

- **Flexibility and efficiency of use**   Accelerators—unseen by the novice user—can often speed up the interaction for the expert user such that the system can cater to both inexperienced and experienced users. Allow users to tailor frequent actions.

- **Aesthetic and minimalist design**   Dialogues should not contain information that is irrelevant or rarely needed. Every extra unit of information in a dialogue competes with the relevant units of information and diminishes their relative visibility.

- **Help users recognize, diagnose, and recover from errors**   Error messages should be expressed in plain language (no codes), precisely indicate the problem, and constructively suggest a solution.

- **Help and documentation**   Even though it is better if the system can be used without documentation, it might be necessary to provide help and documentation. Such information should be easy to search, be focused on the user's task, list concrete steps to be carried out, and not be too large.

Unfortunately, heuristic evaluations have a spotty track record: they can be hard to apply, the results are inconsistent, and most teams prefer usability studies. **Evaluations are only as good as the heuristics themselves, and the popular heuristics are well beyond their "best by" date. Nielsen's are over 25 years old, hard to apply, and of questionable relevance to modern apps.**

Tweet This!

Modern heuristic evaluations

To make design heuristics effective, they must be useful (find real problems), important (find problems people care about), relevant (apply to current technology), understandable (their meaning is clear), and objective (clearly distinguish problems from nonproblems). Sound familiar? **The Eight Attributes of Intuitive UI operate this way, so you can use them for effective heuristic evaluations.**

Here's a process for performing a team-based intuitive heuristic evaluation for a specific UI:

1. **Start with scenarios**   As a team (typically 3–5 evaluators), determine a small number of important scenarios that involve the UI. Make sure each scenario clearly explains who is using it, why they are using it (their goal), and where they are using it.

2. **Apply the heuristics**   Individually, have each team member perform the scenario with the UI and ask the following heuristic questions based on the Eight Attributes of Intuitive UI:

    a. Based on the target users' context and what's on the screen, will users quickly **discover** the features they are looking for?

    b. Is the interaction obvious based on the **affordances**? Will target users perform the interaction right the first time, or will they resort to trial and error?

    c. Is the label **comprehensible** to the target users? Does the label assist discoverability and setting expectations, or will target users resort to trial and error to figure it out? Will target users know how to decide and respond based on what they already know?

    d. Once the user initiates the interaction, is there **responsive feedback**? Is it immediately obvious *in context* that the command has taken effect? Is it obvious that the interaction has succeeded, has failed, or is still in progress?

e. Will target users accurately **predict** the results of the interaction? Do the results (including any side effects) meet their **expectations**, or are they surprised? (A simple way to determine: When evaluating, predict the results before performing the interaction, and then compare with the actual results.)

f. Is the interaction **efficient**? Are there any obviously unnecessary steps or repetition? Are appropriate defaults provided? Could anything be performed automatically instead of manually? If you repeat the step, is it easier to perform the second time?

g. Is the interaction **forgiving**? Purposely make small mistakes at each step to determine what happens. Is it easy to recover, or do users have to start over?

h. Will target users feel **confident** in the outcome of the interaction? Will users feel able to **explore** the interaction without making a serious mistake or resulting in unintended consequences? Is there a clear commitment point where users are *certain* the task is complete, and can users easily abandon the task before that point?

3. **Score using Pass/Fail** Score on a simple Pass/Fail basis, as described earlier in this chapter. If an intuitive attribute is missing, that's a problem.

4. **Compare results** When done, compare results and agree on the problems found as well as the heuristics/intuitive attributes behind each problem.

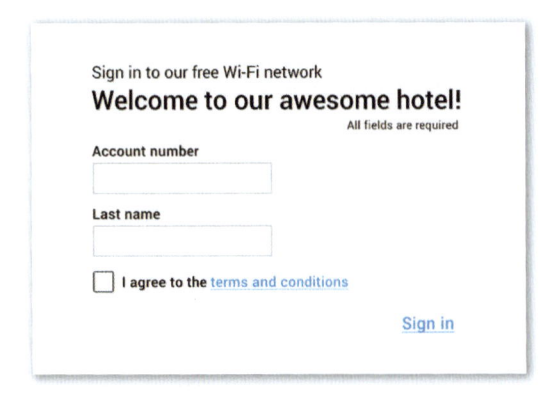

FIGURE 7-4 A free Wi-Fi sign-in screen for a hotel.

Let's now work through the heuristics for this sign-in screen:

1. **Discoverability** Everything is easily discoverable. **Pass!**

2. **Affordance** The "Sign in" command is a link instead of a button—which might be appropriate for a secondary command but not a primary one—making the primary interaction less obvious. **Fail.** (Harsh, I know, but remember our goal is to improve the design.)

3. **Comprehensible**   All labels are comprehensible. However, the form is asking for the user's account number, which they are unlikely to know from memory. It should ask for the user's email address or name instead. **Fail.**

4. **Responsive feedback**   Both success and failure are immediately obvious. **Pass!**

5. **Predictable**   The results are easily predictable. **Pass!**

6. **Efficiency**   If the user's email address were used instead of the account number, it could be filled in by default. **Fail.**

7. **Forgiving**   If the user makes a mistake, the input fields are cleared and the user has to start over. Furthermore, it's impossible for the user to review the input to determine the problem. Contrary to popular belief, clearing the input fields is not necessary to prevent information disclosure. **Fail.**

8. **Confidence and explorability**   No problems found. **Pass!**

To summarize, we applied each of the Eight Attributes of Intuitive UI as design heuristics. As a result, we found that we can improve this sign-in UI by giving the "Sign In" command a button affordance, asking questions the target users can easily answer (and providing nonprivate information by default), and not clearing on error. **After doing this quick heuristic evaluation, any subsequent usability testing will be far more productive.**

> *You can perform effective heuristic evaluations by using the Eight Attributes of Intuitive UI as heuristics.*

Tweet This!

Streamlined Cognitive Walkthroughs

One of my favorite expert evaluation techniques is the *Streamlined Cognitive Walkthrough (SCW)*, a group activity that evaluates the intuitiveness of a design and its task flow by asking a set of questions at each step. The questions are

1. How will users know what to do at this step?
2. If users do the right thing, how will they know?
3. If users do the wrong thing, how will they know?
4. If users do the wrong thing, how will they correct the problem?

The first two questions were devised by Rick Spencer to streamline the process, but I added the last two questions to force the evaluation off the *happy path*—where users are assumed

to perform tasks perfectly. Often teams evaluate their own designs by assuming users know and stay on the happy path, which is completely unrealistic for all but the most trivial tasks.

More important, these questions map extremely well to the Eight Attributes of Intuitive UI (only *efficiency* is missing). Instead of evaluating the attributes directly, as with a heuristic evaluation, a Streamlined Cognitive Walkthrough evaluates intuitiveness from a different perspective. Here's the mapping:

- **How will users know what to do at this step?** Evaluates discoverability, affordance, comprehensibility, and predictability.
- **If users do the right thing, how will they know?** Evaluates responsive (positive) feedback.
- **If users do the wrong thing, how will they know?** Evaluates responsive (negative) feedback.
- **If users do the wrong thing, how will they correct the problem?** Evaluates forgiveness and explorability.

Even more important: a Streamlined Cognitive Walkthrough is a great way to convince your executive team that there's a problem with the intuitiveness of your product. Do an SCW with your executive team for a variety of scenarios so that they can draw conclusions themselves. *Executives never argue with their own conclusions*, so they are more likely to be persuaded by participating in an SCW than any other evaluation. If your execs have trouble performing basic tasks with their own product, that usually gets their attention. Never underestimate the power of direct personal experience (with a touch of embarrassment).

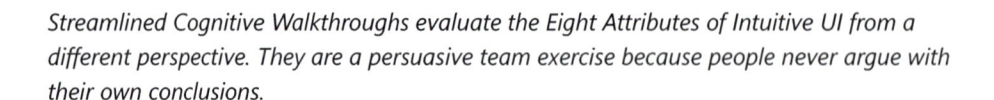

Tweet This!

> *Streamlined Cognitive Walkthroughs evaluate the Eight Attributes of Intuitive UI from a different perspective. They are a persuasive team exercise because people never argue with their own conclusions.*

Let work through an example.

> *Let's request a ride using Uber, assuming that the user is in an unfamiliar city (NYC) and would like a ride from a train station to a hotel.*

This task requires three steps: 1) Setting the pickup location, 2) setting the destination, and 3) making the request.

(Please bear in mind that I'm evaluating how Uber works at the time of this writing (2017), so it may be quite different now.)

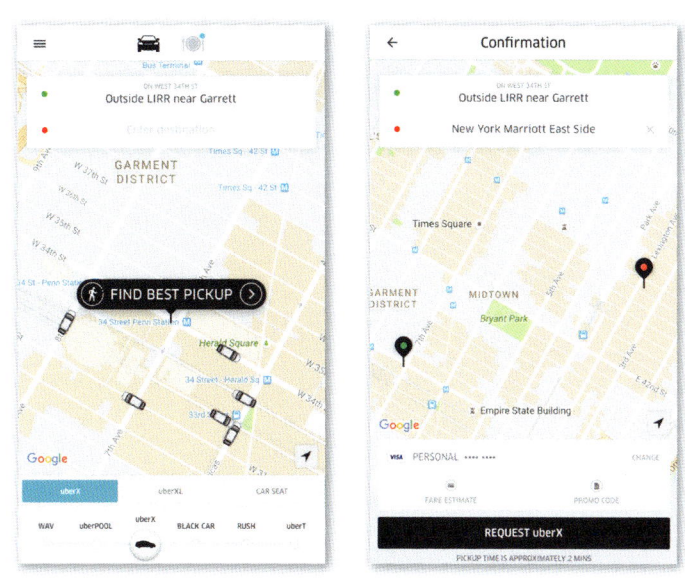

FIGURE 7-5 Two screens for the three steps for requesting a ride using Uber in New York City.

Let's work through the SCW questions:

1. How will users know what to do at this step?

    a. **Step 1** Users will know to set the pickup location if 1) they know their address or 2) the GPS location is accurate. The explicit Find Best Pickup button makes this step easily discoverable. Otherwise, the "green" text box is unlabeled by default, so users have to deduce that this is the pickup location.

    b. **Step 2** Users must enter their destination in the "red" text box, and they must know that the red color is not an error. Users can enter either a specific address or the name of a landmark, so they don't have to know the exact address. **[Potentially unintuitive]**

    c. **Step 3** Users have to know to tap the uberX option. If that option currently isn't available, they have to choose another option or they must know to wait. Neither is explicitly explained in the UI. **[Not intuitive!]**

2. If users do the right thing, how will they know?

    a. **Step 1** Users will be able to confirm their location with the map, their GPS location on the map, and the address in the "green" text box, which requires either an accurate GPS location, clear street signs, or obvious landmarks.

    b. **Step 2** There is no visual feedback that shows the destination location until Step 3 is complete. **[Potentially unintuitive]**

c. **Step 3**   The screen changes slightly to reveal an explicit "REQUEST uberX" button.

3. If users do the wrong thing, how will they know?

    a. **Step 1**   Users will know they made a mistake if they recognize where they are on the map or notice the absence of the blue GPS location dot. If users make a mistake (by requesting a pickup location they aren't physically at), there is no warning. **[Not intuitive!]**

    b. **Step 2**   There is no visual feedback that shows the destination location until Step 3 is complete. **[Potentially unintuitive]**

    c. **Step 3**   The "REQUEST uberX" button will not be revealed, but users will have to deduce the problem, because there is no instruction or message. **[Potentially unintuitive]**

4. If users do the wrong thing, how will they correct the problem?

    a. **Step 1**   Before requesting the ride, they can tap the "green" text box to reset the location. After ordering, they can cancel the ride, perhaps with a penalty.

    b. **Step 2**   Before requesting the ride, they can tap the "red" text box to reset the destination. After ordering, they can cancel the ride, perhaps with a penalty.

    c. **Step 3**   Users must eventually figure out that they need to tap an uber option. If they choose the wrong option (uberPool vs. uberX), they can change this by tapping the Back button.

As you can see, a good Streamlined Cognitive Walkthrough quickly reveals problems with unintuitive UI, and using the SCW's four questions helps you find problems in your own design without looking past them. Doing so before usability testing will make it much more productive. But be sure to get off that happy path!

By the way, I chose this example deliberately because I have personally made the mistakes pointed out here. More explicit labeling, instructions, and steps, plus giving a warning when users make an obvious pickup location mistake, would really help make this simple task more intuitive.

Usability testing

Successful usability testing is the least subjective measure of intuitive design. After all, we can agree that our own designs are fantastically intuitive, but none of that matters if actual target users can't get real tasks done. In case you aren't familiar with usability testing, it is just that: evaluating the usability of a design by having several target users try to perform realistic tasks—on their own—either in a usability lab, in an office, or remotely over the internet. (As I've mentioned, many people consider six participants to be the optimal number.)

FIGURE 7-6 A typical informal usability test.

(While often referred to as *user testing*, *usability testing* makes it clear that you are testing the design, not the person—an important distinction.)

Usability testing is the ultimate measure, but **it's fairly time- and labor-intensive. Here's a summary of the steps involved:**

1. Determine the goal of the study and metrics for success.
2. Have something to test (such as the real product, prototype, or MVP).
3. Create a list of tasks for users to perform that achieves the goals of the study.
4. Set up the test environment; do a trial run to find and fix problems.
5. Recruit participants from real target users.
6. Perform the study; record the results.
7. Analyze the results; make a list of recommended changes.

That's a lot of work and often we just don't have the time, even if we have user research talent and cut some corners. This is why I recommend both usability testing and expert evaluation, so that you can focus usability testing on the hard-to-find problems and get as much value out of the process as possible.

Going into usability testing (formal or informal) in detail is beyond the scope of this book, but if you're interested in learning more about the process, I recommend the *Handbook of Usability*

Testing, by Jeffrey Rubin and Dana Chisnell, and *Rocket Surgery Made Easy,* by Steve Krug. That said, I have three bits of advice that you won't find anywhere else.

Tip 1: Choose metrics that measure intuitiveness in a meaningful way. *Success rates* measure overall intuitiveness, and *task completion times* measure efficiency directly and the other attributes indirectly. Consider measuring other factors that also indicate intuitiveness. I like to track what I call *botched interactions*, where users make small mistakes that they ultimately correct, perhaps very quickly. Another is what I call *awkward pauses*, where the user stops the task flow, perhaps to ask a question or express confusion. Both of these metrics reveal intuitiveness problems that success rates and completion times might gloss over.

Tip 2: Map your study results to the Eight Attributes of Intuitive UI—most importantly, using their vocabulary (*discoverability*, *affordance*, etc.) to describe the findings and recommended changes. Doing so makes it easier to have discussions with your team and reveals patterns in the design problems you find. They likely aren't random!

Tip 3: Don't be surprised if missing any of the Eight Attributes of Intuitive UI leads to usability problems. I see designers cut corners with poor discoverability, poor labeling/comprehensibility, or poor feedback, expecting that their absence won't be a problem. It almost always is—exceptions are rare. Put it on the screen! Have the affordance! Add the extra word or two! Give clear feedback! Get off that happy path to see what's really happening!

The User Manual Highlighter Test

As I mentioned in Chapter 1, user manuals often do little more than document all the unintuitive UI in an app. **A simple, yet effective way to evaluate your designs is to review your documentation (both the manuals and the online Help) to find explanations of unintuitive UI that potentially could be eliminated through design improvements.** Highlight these as you go, and then perform a design review to propose design changes.

Many users believe that Help isn't helpful—and they are right. Too often, Help documents how UI elements work mechanically. I call this Null Help, which explains, among other things, that you need to type text into text boxes, choose an option from a group of option buttons, click Cancel to cancel the task…and oh yeah, click Help for more information. In other words, such unhelpful help tells you what you already know—even if you don't know anything. Consider this gem:

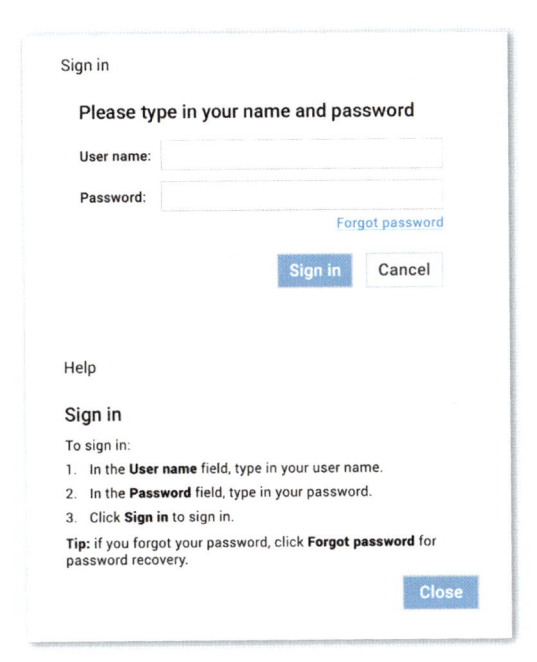

FIGURE 7-7 OK, got it! That helps!

Let's look at a simple example for creating a user account.

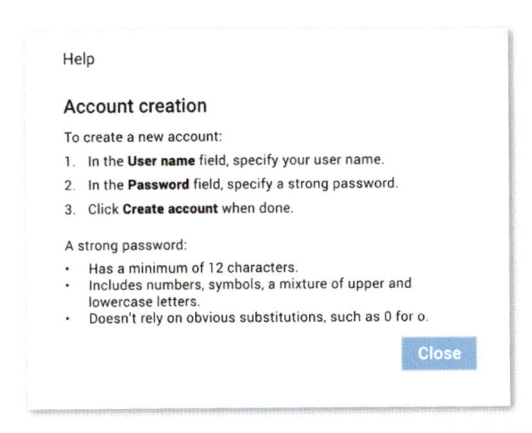

FIGURE 7-8 Help for creating a user account. Is this Help helpful?

This Help explains only one useful thing: the strong password restrictions. By putting this important information directly on the page, we can make that Help information redundant. Now all that remains is Null Help, so we can eliminate the entire Help screen.

User manuals and Help often do little more than document unintuitive UI. Leverage this by reviewing your documentation and Help to see what can be eliminated through small design improvements. You will be surprised by how much can.

Summary

In this chapter, you learned some tools and techniques for designing intuitive UI as part of your existing design process. Because nearly all design decisions require approval, you can use the Seven Levels of UX Persuasion to help you choose the appropriate level to persuade team members, managers, stakeholders, and clients.

Using usability testing on your designs to check for intuitiveness is very objective, but you can use heuristic evaluations and Streamlined Cognitive Walkthroughs to find the more *obvious* problems, which in turn makes any usability testing you do far more productive and your overall process much more efficient. You can use the User Manual Highlighter Test to see how well you've done and to find ways to do even better.

Exercises

Apply what you have learned in this chapter with the following exercises:

1. Choose a UI design to either defend or challenge, and try to persuade someone else of your position. Start by using personal opinion alone. Were you successful? If not, refer to the Seven Levels of Persuasive UX and choose appropriate higher levels. Were you more successful?

2. For a single, simple UI, gather two teams of designers and have one perform a heuristic evaluation using Nielsen's usability heuristics and have the other team perform an evaluation based on the Eight Attributes of Intuitive UI, as described in this chapter. Give both teams a suitable time limit based on the UI. Compare the results. Which technique resulted in better findings?

3. For a simple unintuitive UI, perform a Streamlined Cognitive Walkthrough and a usability study. Compare the results. Devise a simple strategy for when to use these techniques.

4. Repeat Exercise 3 for an intuitive UI. Does this experiment change your strategy?

Conclusion

As a modern UX designer, a crucial part of your job is to design UIs that your target users can understand immediately on their own, without reasoning, experimenting, memorizing, training, or reading documentation. Your users expect this now, and they are no longer motivated to spend time learning your app, reading documentation, or getting training.

You now know what it means to be intuitive (by definition), the specific attributes required to make a UI intuitive, and how to evaluate intuitiveness without relying solely on user testing. That said, you appreciate that not everything needs to be intuitive as other design tradeoffs might be more important, and you know how to make those tradeoffs strategically rather than accidentally. You have a better vocabulary that you can use to discuss intuitive UI with your team persuasively, without resorting to subjective personal opinion, analogies, or metaphors.

You also understand that ultimately a UI is intuitive only if your target users demonstrate that it is by performing the top tasks smoothly and effortlessly. The goal of this book isn't to replace usability testing, but to make it—as well as your overall design process—more effective and less expensive.

Remember the *Manifestation of Intuitive UI*: You observe that users successfully complete tasks on the first try consistently, without making mistakes. If that's not the case for your app's important interactions, you have more work to do.

Glossary

Oh happy vague, abstract design lingo. This is thy definition!

Above the fold Content that users can see without any scrolling. Originates from newspapers, where "above the fold" refers to the top half of a folded newspaper that can be seen when in a stack.

Affordance A visual property of a UI element that suggests the element is interactive, and how to interact with it. For example, push buttons look like real-world buttons that are pushed to activate. If an affordance is successful, users don't have to experiment or deduce how to perform an interaction. Affordance can be assessed through clear visual clues that are consist with the target user's prior experience, and formally through click testing.

Below the fold Content that requires scrolling to see. The opposite of *above the fold*.

Coach marks A brief overview of the commands available on a screen. Similar to onboarding, but coach marks explain the interactions for a single screen on demand.

Cognitive (work)load Formally, the portion of the user' mental capabilities required to perform a task. Designers should make sure that the required cognitive load realistically matches known human capabilities in context.

Cognitive walkthrough A team-based "expert" usability inspection method that walks through a task step by step, and evaluating intuitiveness by asking several questions at each step. A streamlined Cognitive Walkthrough (SCW) reduces the number of questions.

Commit model The interaction model that determines how changes are committed or discarded and how users navigate to the next step in a task. The most common commit models are explicit save and instant commit.

Commit buttons Commands used for saving or discarding user changes and navigating to the next step. Common commit buttons include OK, Cancel, Save, and Close.

Comprehensibility Target users' ability to understand the meaning and effect of a UI element—enough to recognize that it is the right element for the desired task, to understand what the element does, and to make the right choices while interacting with it.

Confusion An inconsistency in UI that leads users to draw incorrect conclusions about system state, interaction, or effect. For example, a control that looks like a push button is confusing when it is activated on a swipe.

Consistency Conformity of appearance and behavior within an application or across applications. "Good" consistency helps make UIs easier to use and more intuitive by leveraging existing knowledge and making interactions more discoverable and predictable. (By contrast, "bad" consistency is consistency for its own sake, and often undermines these goals.)

Constraints Restrictions that limit input to valid values. Good constraints make it easier for users to achieve their goals and less likely to make mistakes.

Dark pattern A design technique where designers purposely manipulate or even trick users into doing something (buying, upgrading, accepting unfavorable terms and conditions) against their best interest.

Deductive UI A task that requires users to think and experiment, often using the process of elimination to figure out; or alternatively refer to documentation.

Delighter A strategically unintuitive interaction that delights expert users on discovery. Delighters reward expert users for their expertise. Well-designed delighters enhance the experience for experts without harming the experience for everyone else.

Design model The designers' intention for how they believe a product should work, which may differ from how it actually works (the *system image*) or how users' interpretations of how they think it works (the *user model*.) Unintuitive UIs often lead to inaccurate user models.

Direct manipulation When users interact directly with an object's representation on the screen, as opposed to indirectly through some UI proxy (like a menu, dialog box, or command line). But where there is direct manipulation, there is the potential for *accidental manipulation*.

Discoverability Target users' ability to locate the UI elements needed to achieve a goal—when they need them. Discoverability can be measured by task completion times or eye tracking.

Efficiency For intuitive interaction, efficiency determines whether the design helps target users perform their top tasks with unnecessary interaction or repetition.

Explorability Determines whether target users can use an app without fear of getting lost or making significant mistakes. Top causes for poor explorability are confusing, nonstandard navigation models and unclear, nonstandard commit models. A good antonym for explorable is *hazard-prone*.

Explainable first A design process where designers start a page design by making its purpose easily explainable to users, often by determining a main instruction for the page. By doing so, users are more likely to figure out such pages on their own, making the resulting task flows intuitive.

Expert evaluation A process for evaluating a design through inspection methods performed by "experts" (likely team members, not real users). While not as dependable as usability testing, expert evaluations can be focused and detailed, and quick to perform.

Familiarity An assessment to whether target users can apply previously learned knowledge to the current interaction. Successfully doing so requires *consistency* with those prior interactions, otherwise users will be misled or confused.

Feedback A clear, accurate indication of the current state of an interaction or the resulting state. If an interaction has completed, users need a clear indication of completion and whether it succeeded or failed. Most feedback needs to be *responsive* to be useful.

Forgiveness Assesses whether an interaction prevents mistakes, minimizes the negative impact of mistakes, or makes mistakes easy to recover from. Intuitive apps assume that small mistakes are common, and they accommodate these mistakes. By contrast, unintuitive apps are not forgiving and result in a significant loss of work or inconvenience, such as forcing the user to completely redo the task.

Fully intuitive An interaction that has all the necessary Eight Attributes of Intuitive UI. As a result, the interaction is immediately self-explanatory and most users can perform it without any problems.

Gesture A direct touch-based interaction with an object or content. While *sensible* gestures are obvious from inspection, *learnable* gestures require experimentation and memorization because they lack discoverability or affordance.

Guessable An interaction that is usable but not fully intuitive because it is missing several intuitive attributes. While they aren't as obvious as sensible or learnable, users learn them through experience and are eventually able to guess accurately where to find them or how they work.

Hamburger menu A menu commonly associated with responsive web design and mobile apps that concisely displays commands and navigation options. So called because the three horizontal line icon typically used resembles a hamburger.

Happy path The ideal task flow, where users are assumed to perform each step perfectly. Except for trivial tasks, most paths aren't nearly that happy so in practice users end up on an often poorly designed *unhappy path*.

Happy path myopia Occurs when teams unrealistically evaluate their designs only by looking at the happy path—and therefore assume that users never make mistakes.

Hero image A large, prominent banner image, typically at the top of a page.

Heuristics (usability) A set of recognized (by independent parties) usability principles.

Heuristic evaluation A team-based "expert" usability inspection method that evaluates a design based on compliance with established design heuristics.

Important/unimportant interactions In this book, an interaction is described as *important* if it's needed by most users for routine tasks. By contrast, an unimportant interaction is advanced, infrequent, or optional, and therefore isn't a significant problem if not fully intuitive.

Inductive UI A task that leads users through easily explainable, self-explanatory steps, reducing the need for users to think and experiment to perform the steps. Put more simply, inductive UIs enable intuitive multi-step tasks. By contrast, deductive tasks require users to think and experiment, often using the process of elimination to figure out.

Inspection method A team-based "expert" design evaluation process where the evaluators apply a usability evaluation process or set of usability heuristics.

Instinctive The typical dictionary definition of *intuitive* is *instinctive*, which means knowledge or behavior people are born with. For *intuitive UI*, it's more helpful to consider users' prior knowledge regardless of when it was acquired.

Interaction lifecycle The sequence of steps—both mental and physical—that a user performs to complete a task.

Intuitive A user interface is intuitive when target users understand its behavior and effect without use of reason, memorization, experimentation, assistance, or training. An intuitive UI is immediately self-explanatory to its target users. An unintuitive UI may be highly usable, but will require some effort from users and therefore its adaption is dependent upon users giving that effort.

Invisible UI A well designed UI where users are immersed in their work, and not thinking about the UI at all—making the UI feel as if it were invisible.

Learnable An interaction that is usable but not fully intuitive because it lacks discoverability or affordance. Learnable interactions aren't as obvious as sensible ones and they require some thought or experimentation, but they are often considered by users to be intuitive once learned. Called learnable because they are often learned by observing others.

Long press A touch-based interaction that is like a tap, but the user maintains contact longer than a normal tap. Often called tap and hold, but long press is more accurate.

Main instruction A heading that explicitly explains what users are supposed to do on a page. So called because it describes the entire page rather than a portion. Determining main instructions is a useful step in designing intuitive task flows.

Manifestation of intuitive UI An intuitive UI manifests itself when you observe users successfully completing tasks on the first try consistently, without making mistakes. This means intuitive UI is observable and measurable.

Mental model Users' interpretations of how they think a product works, which may differ from how it actually works (the *system image*) or how designers' intention for how it works (the *design model*.) A common synonym for user model.

Misleading An inconsistency in UI element attributes that leads users to draw incorrect conclusions about system state, interaction, or effect. For example, a control that looks like a push button is confusing when it is activated on a swipe.

Natural mapping A clear relationship between what the user wants to do and how they should do it, based on spatial (up naturally maps to more) or cultural (right naturally maps to more in Western cultures) relationships.

Onboarding A brief overview of an app that is displayed on first launch and that often explains how to use its unintuitive features. The goal is to get new users familiar and successful with an app as quickly as possible.

Predictability Whether target users can accurately predict the results of an interaction before they initiate it. An interaction is unpredictable if target users are surprised by the results or any of its side effects. A simple way to evaluate predictability is to ask users to predict the outcome of an interaction before they do it.

Responsive An assessment to whether an event is considered immediate or delayed. Technically, a response time of under 200 ms is perceived as immediate.

Responsive design An approach to web page design that makes use of flexible layouts, flexible images, and cascading style sheet media queries. The goal of responsive design is to build web pages that detect the user's screen size and orientation and change the layout accordingly.

RTFM An acronym for "Read The Fine Manual." RTFM is an attitude in classic UI design that assumes documenting an unintuitive design is a suitable solution (instead of redesigning the UI to eliminate the problem); and if users don't read the manual, their inability to complete a task is their fault. By contrast, modern, intuitive UI design assumes that users won't read manuals and shouldn't have to.

Scannability An assessment to whether target users can find what they are looking for quickly—ideally at a glance.

Section instruction A heading that explicitly explains the purpose of a section on a responsive page. These instructions help keep users oriented as they scroll.

Sensible An interaction that is usable but not fully intuitive because it lacks discoverability or affordance. While they require trivial thought and experimentation, sensible interactions are so natural that users figure them out quickly and consider them to be intuitive.

Shortcut An advanced interaction, usually requiring experimentation and memorization, that lets experienced users perform a task more efficiently. Shortcuts usually lack discoverability or affordance.

Side effect A secondary, possibly unwanted, result of an interaction.

Single-trial learning The concept that some interactions are sufficiently self-explanatory that users learn them after a single trial. However, research shows that users generally retain surprisingly little of what they learn, so a more accurate name might be *multiple-trial forgetting*.

Skeuomorphism The use of decorative, ornamental real-world elements that aren't necessary for the interaction. For example, an address book might have a leather binding (with folds!), stitching, dog eared pages.

Streamlined cognitive walkthrough A team-based "expert" usability inspection method that walks through a task step by step, evaluating intuitiveness by asking a small set of questions at each step.

System image The way a product actually works, which may differ from the way its designers intended it to work (the *design model*) or users' interpretation of how it works (the *user model*.) Unintuitive UIs often lead to inaccurate user models.

Target users A group of users an interaction is expressly designed for. Different target users have different computer and domain knowledge, training, and experience, so intuitive UIs are designed for specific target users. While a walk-up kiosk might be designed for everyone, aircraft avionics are design specifically for trained pilots.

Task flow The presentation of a sequence of steps to perform a multi-step task, either within a page or across pages.

Task lifecycle The sequence of actions—both mental and physical—that a user performs to complete a multi-step task.

Thelma and Louise A multi-step task without a clear, visible ending—the interaction equivalent of driving off a cliff.

Trainable An interaction that is usable but not fully intuitive because it is missing many intuitive attributes. So named because users must resort to training and documentation to use them. Trainable should be avoided as *sensible*, *guessable*, and *learnable* are much better alternatives.

3D Touch A capability that uses the amount of force a user puts on the touch screen to activate different functions, typically to display a menu.

TURD An acronym for *Terrible User experience from Responsive Design*. Describes websites that use the responsive design clichés without any clear user benefit. Avoid these.

Unhappy path A realistic task flow, where users make many mistakes such as providing incorrect input and making poor navigation choices. Users make small mistakes all the time, so unhappy paths should be designed just as carefully as the *happy path*.

Unintuitive An interaction that lacks the required intuitive attributes, so it may require some reasoning, experimentation, memorization, documentation, or training to use. An unintuitive UI isn't necessarily a poor experience and may be considered quite usable, especially if the tradeoffs required to make it intuitive just aren't worth it.

Unusable An interaction so poorly designed that even documentation and training can't make it usable. Expect a lot of tech support calls for these.

Usable A design that is easy to use, perhaps requiring some user effort or even training and documentation. An intuitive design is considered usable, but the reverse isn't necessarily true.

Usability testing A process for evaluating a design by testing it with real users performing real tasks. Considered the most dependable evaluation technique because findings are based upon empirical evidence. While often referred to as *user testing*, *usability testing* makes it clear that you are testing the design, not the person—an important distinction.

User model Users' interpretations of how they think a product works, which may differ from how it actually works (the *system image*) or how designers' intention for how it works (the *design model*.) Unintuitive UIs often lead to inaccurate user models.

What You See Is What You Get (WYSIWYG) A design goal of making what users see in a preview an accurate representation of what they will actually get. Originally referred to on-screen previews matching the printed page.

What You Want Is Bloody Impossible (WYWIBI) An unintuitive UI that makes it difficult or impossible for users to achieve their goals.

Index

A
above the fold 146
accessibility 48
    color confusion (vs. color blindness) 48
accidental manipulation 77
affordance 33–39, 115, 161
    common affordance table 34–36
    cost of 110
    definition 33
    minimal 36
    misleading 37
agile xv
air conditioning 51
airplane crash 103
Android 8, 78
    Android Design Principles 100
    Back, Home, Recents 8
    Calculator app 75
    Clock app 81
    material design 36
    Material Design Guidelines 100
Apple 5, 14
awkward pauses 168

B
Bateman, Donald 12
behaviors
    automatic xviii, 78
    incorrect 50
    instinctive 16
    real-world 33, 120, 124, 156, 160
below the fold 80
Bias, Randolf 4
Blackberry 8
Bluetooth 73

C
calculators 70
Campaign Monitor 149
carets 33
Chisnell, Dana 168
Christensen, Clayton 4
coach marks 125–128
    definition 125
    guidelines 127
cognitive load xviii
collaboration 157
Collins, Jim 5
color
    confusion (vs. color blindness) 48
    status 48
commands
    advanced, infrequent, optional 112, 154
    commit 74, 135
    contextual 28, 29
    destructive, irreversible 115
    frequent vs. infrequent 27
    primary vs. secondary 30
commit models 76, 79, 136
    explicit save 79
    instant commit 79
comprehensibility 40–46, 94, 106, 161
    asking good questions 45
    comprehensibility vs. technical accuracy 40
    cost of 111
    defintion 40
    expectations 42
    labels 43
    speaking the user's language 40
confirmations 76, 103
consistency 34, 97
    definition 97
    expectation of 98
    good vs. bad 100
constraints 63
context 29, 40, 57, 67
controls
    buttons 33, 56
    Cancel buttons 44, 54, 81
    clearing user input 61
    Continue buttons 63
    date pickers 57
    defaults 58–60, 162
    headers (vs. banners) 36
    input formats 64–67
    labels 37, 38, 40, 43, 56, 94, 96, 97, 163
    links 33, 56
    lists 28, 63
    remembering user input 61

    self-explanatory (vs. concise) 43
    sliders 63
    target sizes 55
    target too small 56
    text boxes 33, 36, 85
    text boxes, constrained vs. unconstrained 63
    text box placeholders 86
Cost-Justifying Usability 4
Csíkszentmihályi, Mihály 102
customer experience (CX)
    definition xviii

D

dark patterns 158
dashboards 143
deductive UI 136
default values 58–60, 162
    reasonable probability 59
    when to not provide 60
definition: intuitive UI 15
delighters 114
design flaws 101
design heuristics 160
design models 14
Design of Everyday Things, The 14, 37, 95
design reviews 54, 146
design tradeoffs 109
desktop xix, 9, 36, 49, 116
development costs 112
digestible 13, 106
    definition 106
direct manipulation 76, 77
discoverability 27–32, 94, 115, 161
    cost of 109
    definition 27
    inevitable 113
    presentation 29
    starting points 27
documentation 1, 2, 3, 138, 155, 168
Don't Make Me Think 102, 138
    when to require thought 115, 119
door handles 37, 95
duck
    labeling 98
    looking like 98
    quacking like 98
dumbed down 14, 19
DVD players 29

E

easy to use 14

efficiency 55–68, 162
    appropriate constraints 63
    appropriate defaults 58–60
    contextual stupidity 67
    definition 55
    error handling 62–63
    inefficient interaction 55
    remembering user input 61
    technical failure 64
    unnecessary interaction 57
    unnecessary restrictions 66
Eight Attributes of Intuitive UI xvi, 23–92, 24, 97, 155, 156, 159, 161, 164, 168
    1: discoverability 27–32
    2: affordance 33–39
    3: comprehensibility 40–46
    4: responsive feedback 47–49
    5: predictability 50
    6: efficiency 55–68
    7: forgiveness 69–75
    8: explorability 76–81
    poster 25
Einstein, Albert
    asking the proper question 145
error messages 62, 103
    myths about 62
    repeating 63
    vs. status 63
errors
    prevention 58
Everett's Law of Complex Input 61
Everett's Law of Intuitive UI 129
Everett's Rule for Custom Icons 85
experimentation 115
expert evaluations 153, 160
explainable first 138–139
    definition 138
explaining in person 14, 44
explorability 76–81, 162
    accidental manipulation 77
    building confidence 80
    commit models 79
    definition 76
    destructive actions 76
    navigation models 78
    user in control 78
exposing inappropriate features 109
external checklists 133

F

factory resets 115
familiar xix–xx, 13, 14, 93–97, 159

feedback
    haptic 49
    redundant 49
flow 102, 168
flow stoppers 103
forgiveness 69–75, 162
    cost of 111
    defintion 69
    easy recovery 74
    preventing mistakes 69
    undo 73
frictionless 106
fully intuitive
    definition 120

G

games 119
gamification 119
garage door remote controls 47
gestures 97, 102, 113, 115, 120
    3D Touch 33
    accidental 117
    definition 115
    double tap 77
    edge swipe 77
    long press 33, 70, 77, 78, 114
    nonstandard 126
    pinch 121
    refresh 121
    search 121
    spread 121
    swipe 77, 115
    tap 120
Good to Great: Why Some Companies Make the Leap and Others Don't 5
guessable 121, 123
    definition 121

H

hamburger menu 84, 148
Handbook of Usability 167
happy path 69, 75, 163, 168
    myopia 69
haptic feedback 49
helicopter controls 95–96
Help, online 2, 168
    Null Help 168, 169
hero image 148
heuristic evaluations 160
    modern 161
Honeywell International 12

Humane Interface, The xix, 93

I

icons 40, 43, 97
    a picture isn't worth a thousand words 43
    comprehension test 46
    custom 43, 123
    Everett's Rule for Custom Icons 43, 85, 86
    standard 43
inductive UI 136–138
    intuitive UI vs. deductive UI 136
Inflight Entertainment controller 89
informed decisions 45, 152
Innovator's Dilemma, The 4
inspection methods 153
instinctive 16, 97
instructions 28, 40, 137
interaction lifecycle 23, 50, 133
    attribute overlap 26
    mapping to intuitive attributes 26
    potential problems 24
interactions
    advanced, infrequent, optional 9
    appearance 29
    botched 168
    common idioms 97
    confirming destructive 76
    conventions 110, 120, 124
    error-prone 121
    first time 58
    mistakes 69
    nonstandard 125
    not starting over 74
    primary vs. secondary 33, 38
    repetitive 55
    single vs. multiple selection 66
    standard 120
    target sizes 55
    unnecessary restrictions 66
    user input 61
    user input formats 64–67
intuitive UI
    bonus attributes 93–108
    cost of 109
    definition 13, **15**, 23, 123
    design process 153–170
    Eight attributes. *See* Eight Attributes of Intuitive UI
    for target users 111
    framework xx
    fully intuitive 120
    grading 156

impractical definitions 13, 93–108
in stressful situations 104
"intuitive once you learn it" excuse 9, 101
missing attributes 97
"our users are trained professionals" excuse 6
"people can learn" excuse 8
"personal and subjective" excuse 6, 159
saves lives 7, 12, 91, 103
seven good reasons for unintuitive UI 112, 129
strategically unintuitive UI 109–131
task flows 133–152
"the best UI is no UI" myth 103
top excuses 6
unintuitive by definition 15, 115, 125
unintuitive by design 102
vs. highly efficient 7
vs. radical innovation 8
invisible 102
iOS 8, 104, 115
    Clock app 56
    Human Interface Guidelines 100
    Voice Command 49
IP addresses 60
iPhone 14, 49, 70, 73
    Home button 8, 70

K

Krug, Steve 102, 138, 168
    instructions must die 138

L

labels
    multiword 43
Law of the Internet User Experience 97
layout 29, 30
    group boxes 30
    panes 30
    separators 29, 30
    showing relationships 30
learnable 1, 14, 101–102, 121, 123, 159
    definition 121
    vs. intuitive 102
learning
    single-trial 122–123
LEDs 99
    flashing 48
Levels of Intuitiveness 122, 154, 155, 156
    Levels of Intuitiveness chart 119–122
    scoring 124
light switches 94

M

magic escalator of acquired knowledge 159
main instructions 139–141
    definition 139
    "manage" is vague 143
    process for designing 140, 143
    when to display 145–148
Manifestation of Intuitive UI 16
margin icons xvii
Mayhew, Brenda 4
mechanical usability 44, 140, 168
memorization 45, 115
mental models 51
menus 116
metaphors 106
Microsoft 5, 9, 36
minimal viable products (MVPs) 112, 167
mobile xviii
mobile apps 2, 3, 114, 125
Molich, Rolf 23, 160
monochrome 49

N

natural 106, 120
    explaining in person 14, 44
natural mapping 52, 96, 102
    definition 52
navigation
    Back 74, 81
    nonstandard models 76
    web-style 78
Nielsen, Jakob 23, 97, 153, 160
Norman, Donald xviii, 14, 37, 46, 95, 125
Norman doors 37, 95

O

obvious always wins 14, 36
onboarding 28, 125–128
    definition 125
    selling value (vs. explaining unintuitive UI) 128

P

pages
    dashboards 143
    instructions 137
    integrity 141–143
    main instructions 139–141
    purpose 136
    self-explanatory 136, 138

state 54
titles 137
Panasonic 98
passwords 41
performance 111
personal and subjective
 "personal and subjective" excuse xix
personal opinion xvi, xix, 10, 13, 106, 124, 156, 158
personas 158
persuasion xvi, 10, 106, 159, 164
platform guidelines 41, 78, 100, 156, 160
predictability 50–54, 94, 161
 cost of 111
 definition 50
 flat-out wrong 50
 misunderstanding 51
 side effects 53
presentation 96
preventing mistakes 69
process of elimination 137
puzzles 119, 138

R

Raskin, Jef xix, 93
Read The Fine Manual (RTFM) 2
recognition 43
redundancy 80
remote controls 98
requiring thought 102, 137
research data 158
responsive design 146, 148
 terrible UX from (TURDs) 148
responsive feedback 47–49, 161
 definition 47
 interaction feedback 47
 status feedback 48
 vs. laggy 47
Rocket Surgery Made Easy 168
Rubin, Jeffrey 168

S

scanability 106, 149
scenarios 158, 161
screen clutter 109, 110
screen grabs 121
scrolling 57, 80
scrum xv
search 52, 65
 design example 84–88
 handling variations and misspellings 65
 returning closest matches 65

section instructions 149
security and privacy 114
 information disclosure 114
self-explanatory 15
sensible 120, 123
 definition 120
Seven Levels of UX Persuasion 157–158
shortcuts 97, 102, 113, 115
 definition 115
short task timeout 105
shower controllers 82, 101–102
side effects 50, 53, 53–54, 78, 161
 definition 53
sign-in screen 162
single-trial learning 122–123
 vs. multiple-trial forgetting 123
skeuomorphism 36
Skype 64
smooth 106
 definition 16
Snapchat 9
sound 49
Spencer, Rick 163
status
 activity indicator 48, 86
 color 48, 99
 feedback 48
 indicators 99
 progress indicator 48
status bars 49
status feedback 160
strategically unintuitive
 summary 128
streamlined cognitive walkthroughs (SCWs) 163–166
stressful situations 104
success metrics 167
 success rates 168
 task completion times 168

T

task flows 133–152
 potential problems 136
task lifecycle 133–135, 136
 potential problems 136
tasks
 abandoning 54
teamwork 10, 88, 106, 154, 159, 164
testing 168
text
 abbreviations 41
 acronyms 41

ambiguous 41
  bold 34
  capitalization 65
  italics 34
  jargon 41
  misleading 41
  punctuation 65
  titles 137
  whitespace 65
tooltips 116
touch xviii, 56, 77, 79, 115
trainable 121, 123
  definition 121
training 1, 3, 138, 155
TURDs 148

U

Uber 164–166
UI elements
  target sizes 55
UI vs. UX xviii
Undo 73, 76, 79
  broad interpretation 74
  making predictable 73
United Nations Conventions on Road Signs and Signals 48, 99
usability 160
Usability Engineering 160
usability heuristics 23
usability testing 23, 46, 54, 68, 75, 102, 159, 166–168
  maximizing value 153
  number of participants 153
  vs. expert evaluations 154, 167
  vs. user testing 167
user experience (UX)
  definition xviii
  quality bar 3
  return on investment (ROI) 3
user input
  clearing 87
  not clearing 74
user interface (UI)
  command line 89
  definition xviii
  voice driven 89, 103
user manuals 2, 3, 133
  highlighter test 168
  indicating unintuitive UI 15
user models 14
users
  changing knowledge 124
  confidence 76

emotion 158
expectations 3, 40, 42, 50, 51, 95, 161
experts 19, 20
fear of getting lost 76
first question all users have 134
habituation 76
human error 69
intermediate 20
knowledge 94
knowledge in the world (vs. knowledge in the head) 46
misunderstanding 51
motivated, trained 122
next generation 3, 16
non-native speakers 19
novice 20
prior experience 50, 97
prior knowledge 16, 40, 97, 156
rewarding experts 114
satisfaction 158
sophistication spectrum 20
speaking their language 40, 53
ultimate praise 13
user error 103
user models xviii

V

value propositions 158
Verzi, Robert 153
vibration 49
video record button 105
visual metaphors 33
vocabulary xvi, 93, 106, 157, 159, 168

W

Walter, Aaron 153
Where's Waldo? 119
Wi-Fi 40, 104, 162
Windows
  Start Menu 9, 27, 36
  Windows 8 9, 36
WordPerfect 1
Wroblewski, Luke 36

Y

YouTube 2

About the author

Everett McKay is Principal of UX Design Edge and a UX design trainer and consultant with global clientele. Everett's specialty is finding practical, intuitive, simple, highly usable solutions quickly for web, mobile, and desktop applications. Everett has over 30 years' experience in user interface design and has delivered UX design workshops to an international audience that includes Europe (UK, Ireland, Poland, Greece, Turkey), Asia (India, China), South America (Argentina, Brazil), and Africa (South Africa, Nigeria, Cameroon).

In addition to this book, Everett is author of **UI Is Communication: How to Design Intuitive, User Centered Interfaces by Focusing on Effective Communication**, which provides a groundbreaking approach to user interface interaction and visual design using human communication-based principles and techniques. While at Microsoft, Everett wrote the Windows UX Guidelines for Windows Vista and Windows 7 (but not for Windows 8!).

Everett McKay after his closing keynote at World Usability Day Silesia, Poland 2015.

Everett holds Master of Science and Bachelor of Science degrees in Electrical Engineering and Computer Science from the Massachusetts Institute of Technology.

Stay in touch with Everett through these channels:

- Email: *everettm@intuitiveuibook.com*
- Web: *http://www.uxdesignedge.com*
- Facebook: *https://www.facebook.com/UxDesignEdge*
- LinkedIn: *https://www.linkedin.com/in/everettmckay*
- Twitter: *@uxdesignedge*

You can also join Everett's mailing list at uxdesignedge.com and the Intuitive Design LinkedIn group at *https://www.linkedin.com/groups/8589437*.

UX DesignEdge

Want a more intuitive, easy-to-use product, one that users can immediately understand without training or a manual?

Started by Everett McKay in 2010, **UX Design Edge helps technology teams create better user experiences through practical design training and consulting for mobile, web, and desktop applications.** Our specialty is helping software professionals create modern, intuitive, simple, and delightful user experiences by using tools and techniques that fit limited schedules and budgets.

Consider these options:

> ***Eight Steps to an Intuitive UI* is half-day virtual onsite workshop for evaluating your app and get your team proficient with intuitive design.** The first half of the workshop covers the concepts from this book, and the second half is a design review and other exercises that will help you apply those concepts directly to your app. For more information on this and other virtual workshops, check *virtualuxworkshops.com*.

> **The most cost-effective way to engage with UX Design Edge is to have a two-hour team-based remote design review.** When complete, your team will have a better understanding of the top usability problems your customers face, along with practical solutions to them. You'll be amazed by how much of an improvement you can make in only a couple hours. For more information, check *uxdesignreviews.com*.

> **We believe our three-day customized, onsite team-based workshops are the very best available.** These workshops are delivered on site to your team. They focus on practical tools and techniques and use customized exercises created for direct application to your projects—a proven approach that has the most potential for impact. For more information, check *uxdesignworkshop.com*. If you prefer to a lean focus, check out *leanerux.com*.

> **UX Design Edge offers free monthly webinars on provocative UX design subjects.** To review the calendar and register, see *freeuxwebinars.com*.

For more information about UX design training and consulting, contact Everett directly at *everettm@intuitiveuibook.com*.

Got feedback?

I would love to engage with you about the ideas in this book! Please contact me at *everettm@intuitiveuibook.com*. I plan to update this book periodically, so your feedback definitely matters. Also, **I would love to know how this book helps you and your team make better design decisions and more intuitive UIs.**

Please review and recommend this book

If you enjoyed this book and found it helpful, remember that **the ultimate compliment to an author is a positive review on Amazon.** Share your experience and help other designers discover why they should read *Intuitive Design*. Also, share your thoughts about the book on Twitter using #iuibook.

Please consider recommending this book to friends, colleagues, managers, and anyone asking for UX book recommendations—especially those just starting out. If you are a student, let your HCI professors know about this book. I would be honored if it were part of the curriculum.

Have any good intuitive or unintuitive UI examples?

If you have a compelling story of your encounter with intuitive or unintuitive UI, share your experience at the *Intuitive Design* LinkedIn group.

Get the Intuitive Design Heuristics Playing Cards!

Want to get your team onboard with the Eight Attributes of Intuitive UI quickly? Get the Intuitive Design Heuristics Playing Cards, which summarize the most actionable design principles. The suits and ranks in this standard 52-card deck are meaningful to help you prioritize, so an ace of spades problem easily beats a two of clubs.

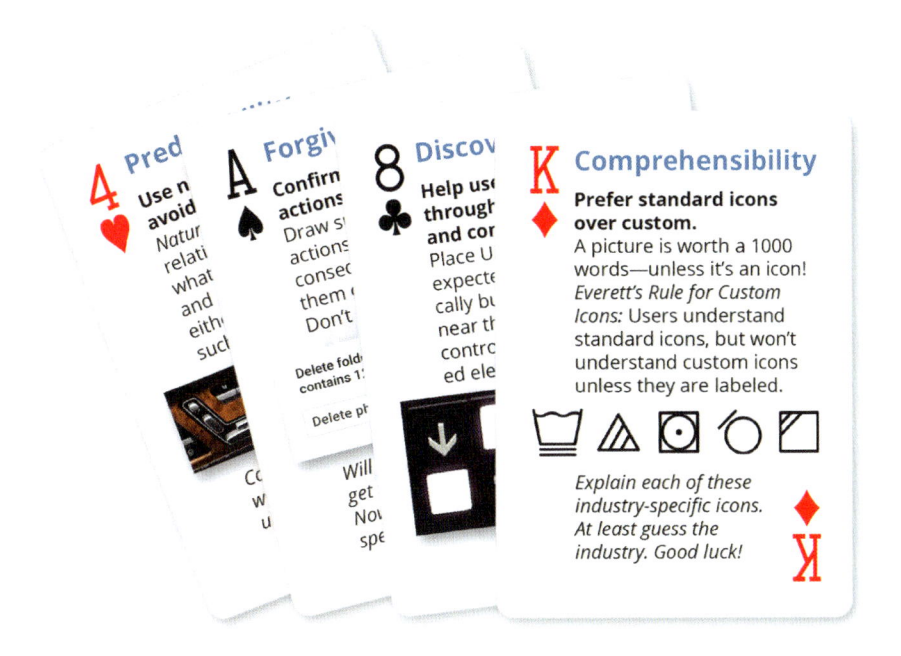

Use these cards to make your design reviews and heuristic evaluations more enjoyable and productive, and help everyone on your team use the same objective, meaningful, actionable design vocabulary based on the Eight Attributes of Intuitive UI. No more design review feedback like "it doesn't feel smooth" or "it needs to be more edgy." (Can a UI even be both smooth and edgy?) The cards make the attributes easier to learn, remember, and use via meaningful games.

For more information and to order, visit *http://uxdesigncards.com.*

The *Intuitive Design* store

Buy a copy of *Intuitive Design* for everyone on your team!

Want to get your team onboard with Intuitive Design? **Buy *Intuitive Design* directly from UX Design Edge to get bulk discounts of signed copies.**

For pricing and to order, check *http://intuitiveuibook.com*.

Attention college instructors

If you are a college professor or lecturer and would like to use Intuitive Design as a textbook, you can license lecture slide decks and videos, plus handouts, lecture notes, workshop exercises, and advanced exercises. Please contact me at *everettm@intuitiveuibook.com* if you are interested.

The Eight Steps to an Intuitive UI Poster

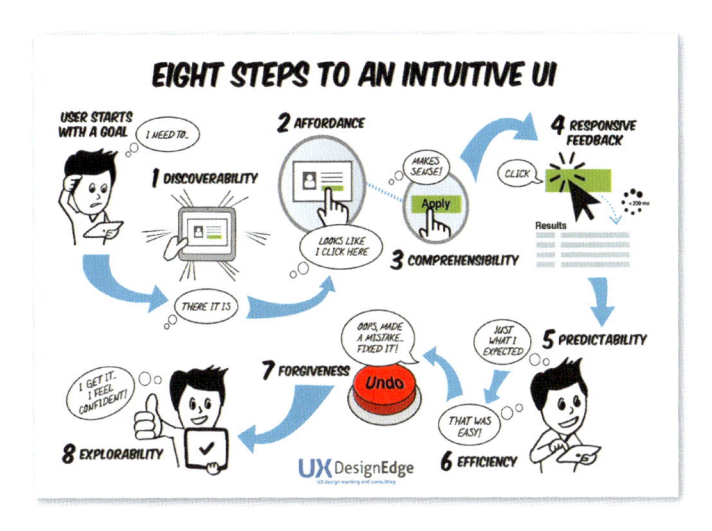

Share the inspiration! This poster is available for sale in various sizes. For size options, pricing, and to order, visit *http://intuitiveuibook.com*.

Printed in Great Britain
by Amazon